Yes Please!
7 Ways to Say
I'm Entitled to the C-Suite

Secrets Women of Color Need to Know Now to Find Their Happy and Win in an Exclusive Corporate Culture

L. MICHELLE SMITH

FOREWORD BY DR. JEFF GARDERE,
"AMERICA'S PSYCHOLOGIST"

Copyright © 2023 no silos communications, LLC

All rights reserved.

ISBN: 978-1-7354706-6-5

DEDICATION

To my smart, beautiful, overachieving, creative, and incredible sister Dr. C. Joyce Price, my best friend, partner in crime, ace, and auntie to Joni.

I see you, and you are amazing. Never forget that.

Thank you for seeing me and being my accomplice.

PRAISE FOR YES PLEASE!

"*Yes Please!* is an absolute must-read for any person looking to demystify ascent to the C-Suite, but more importantly, through authentic storytelling and proven leadership principles exercised by Black women achievers, Yes Please! provides mid-level, mid-career women of color all-important **access** to essential knowledge that is not always readily shared. Thank you, L. Michelle, for this timely work and word."

Xavier Williams
Retired Fortune 10 Executive & CEO, NWS Wireless

"L.Michelle gives you the secrets to navigating the corporate world on your own terms. Anyone who wants to experience higher levels of personal and professional success should read this book."

Trudy Bourgeois
Author of EQUALITY: Courageous Conversations about Women, Men and Race to Spark a Diversity and Inclusion Breakthrough

"L. Michelle is a sister who knows how to help you find success in business."

Toure
Media Personality & Author of Nothing Compares 2 U: An Oral History of Prince

"Using her experience *as **both** a corporate executive and an advisor to Fortune 100 leaders*, and incorporating the stories of fellow Black women professionals, L. Michelle Smith advises high-performing women on surviving – and thriving – on their own journeys to the top. *Yes Please!* is as practical as L. Michelle Smith's other books. Her advice to women about speaking out in a time of great flux in the work world is especially helpful."

**Kristie Bunton, Ph.D.
Dean of the TCU Bob Schieffer College of Communication and author of Having Their Say: Athletes and Entertainers and the Ethics of Speaking Out (McFarland Press, 2021)**

"Once again, L. Michelle has her finger on the pulse of what's going on in corporate America. For me, this book could not have come at a better time. The concept of what we deserve should be required reading for every woman inside and outside of workplaces--and their daughters and nieces. L. Michelle is an important voice in the discussion of work and life, women and people of color, one we should listen to."

**Maria Reeve
Vice President, Texas Initiatives for Hearst,
Former Executive Editor, Houston Chronicle**

"L. Michelle Smith is a passionate advocate and coach for women in the C-Suite. She knows what it takes to open the right doors. If you want to build a confidence and right skill set, *Yes Please!* is the how-to guide you'll keep going back to."

Valorie Burton
National bestselling author of Successful Women Think Differently and CEO of the Coaching and Positive Psychology Institute

Table of Contents

FOREWORD 1

INTRODUCTION 7

1 GUIDING PRINCIPLE: YOU MUST BE HAPPY TO DO THIS, SIS 21

2 AFFIRMATION #1: "I AM LIKABLE AND BRING VALUE TO ANY SPACE" 30

3 AFFIRMATION #2: "I WILL ATTRACT THE RIGHT SPONSORS WHO WILL OPEN DOORS FOR ME" 54

4 AFFIRMATION #3: "I AM WORTHY OF EXECUTIVE COMPENSATION SO THAT I CAN BUILD GENERATIONAL WEALTH" 78

5 AFFIRMATION #4: "I DESERVE A PARTNER WHO RESPECTS, LOVES, AND ADVOCATES FOR ME AND MY LEADERSHIP ASPIRATIONS." 107

6 AFFIRMATION #5: "I DESERVE TO BE HAPPY, SAFE, AND WHOLE ON MY LEADERSHIP JOURNEY." 137

7 AFFIRMATION #6: "I AM A VALUABLE LEADER, AND I WILL BE OPEN TO OTHER ORGANIZATIONS THAT WILL DEMONSTRATE THAT TO ME." 170

8 AFFIRMATION #7: "I AM ENTITLED TO THE ADVOCACY AND MENTORSHIP OF AT LEAST TWO HIGH-POWERED WHITE MEN." 186

9 ONE MORE THING…: A LETTER TO MY BROTHERS 203

10 COACHING GUIDE: 32 POWERFUL QUESTIONS TO LEAD YOU TO HAPPINESS AND THE C-SUITE 210

THE 7 SECRETS CHEAT SHEET: WHAT YOU NEED TO KNOW TO GET TO HAPPY & GET TO THE C-SUITE AS A WOMAN OF COLOR 214

ACKNOWLEDGEMENTS 216

ABOUT THE AUTHOR 219

FOREWORD

I remember meeting L. Michelle by phone back in 2003. We were introduced by a mutual friend who shared a column with her I had written that supplied advice on anything from mental wellness to relationships. From our first conversation, I recognized her keen insight into people and what drives them. She was going through a tough time, but she was thoughtful and empathetic, even to people who may not have treated her well. All this while showing incredible business acumen throughout our conversation.

At the time, she was running her own PR agency, and since then, we not only became friends but we worked together on multiple assignments for some major brands where I was able to share my ability as a practicing forensic psychologist and subject matter expert on national television news and entertainment shows.

Eventually, I became known as "America's Psychologist" after appearing on cable news to chime in on the headlines of some of the biggest crimes, disasters and global events. I've even been featured on some of TV's most-watched reality shows, commenting on family and relationship issues. I'm in the business of understanding and bringing context to human behavior, and that is what particularly excites me about the work L. Michelle is doing as an author and certified executive coach who is trained in the tenets of applied positive psychology and neuroscience. She is one of less than 9% of black executive coaches in the U.S. who are also women and who are credentialed to coach Fortune 500 executives in leadership and personal development. Her ability to back her insights with science is not only unique but sorely needed in a subject matter area that has long gone unaddressed until recently. Namely, the severe lack of women of color, especially Black women leaders in the C-Suites of Fortune 500 companies.

In addition to having had the privilege to work with L. Michelle over the years, I've also watched her career from afar. She is one of the few in this arena who has direct experience in her subject matter, having immersed herself in the stories, lives, and cases of women of color in leadership in corporate America through her international private coaching practice and speaking engagements all over the country. She has personally interacted with the women who are striving and struggling to make it to the top, and she is also one of them. She made vice president before the age of 30 at one of the largest strategic communications firms in the world and became an officer at another global agency not long after running her own boutique agency for about a decade. She has also advised the C-Suite in the Fortune 100 for more than half her career, which spans over 25 years. Throughout this time, she has kept her authenticity, approachability and positive countenance despite the cut-throat nature of the upper ranks in corporate America. She is real, so she keeps it real. You can count on L. Michelle to give it to you straight.

I've found that when the lack of women of color in leadership is addressed, it is typically anecdotal, and the advice comes from heartfelt, yet solely personal experiences. Those accounts are rarely based on research and science. I applaud the voices in this space who are finally providing a platform for this discourse, and I'm incredibly encouraged that L. Michelle has stepped up to bring credible, science-based perspective and actionable leadership insights that I believe will finally create change for the women who have struggled to make it into the C-Suite for far too long.

L. Michelle writes directly to her sisters, intentionally bypassing any real discourse with other decision-makers in corporate America. She counseled corporate leaders on matters of diversity and inclusion at one point in her career, standing up an entire practice in its global marketing organization. While it was rewarding, she said it was also exhausting. After all, why would the oppressed find joy in educating the oppressor? I liken that to telling an abused spouse to educate and change his or her abusive partner. I understand why L. Michelle has finally decided against this. There are a deluge of business books and experts trying to tackle the conundrum and challenge of diversity, equity, inclusion and belonging. L. Michelle honors these warriors, but she chooses a different path. As she adeptly said in her writings, after 50 years of DE&I programs not solving the problems of bias, sexism and racism, there is no more time for women of color to waste on waiting for corporate America to finally get it right.

As with her earlier work, *No Thanks: 7 Ways to Say I'll Just Include Myself, A Guide to Rockstar Leadership for Women of Color in the Workplace*, in which I was proud to take part, L. Michelle not only builds a case for why more women of color belong in the upper echelons of corporate leadership, but she shares how women of color deserve to be in the C-Suite and states unapologetically that they are entitled to be there. She shares how to achieve that goal while weaving in compelling storytelling from her personal experience and that of high-ranking Black women in her own circle of influence. More importantly, like her earlier work, *Yes Please*! is built on the chassis of the core findings of positive psychology, namely that positive emotion and positive self-talk are crucial to anyone's success but especially important for subsets of society who are othered, – those people who happen to be doubly disadvantaged in spaces that center whiteness and maleness, i.e women of color, but most specifically, Black women.

It has been shown through multiple studies, such as those from LeanIn.org, Catalyst, and the Executive Leadership Council, that in addition to a lack of mentorship and sponsorship, these women are not only lacking in the positive feedback that comes from mentors and sponsors but also from themselves, because the constant microaggressions and biases they face on a daily basis make workplace environments ripe with negativity. This negative emotion can be taken on by people who are othered, sometimes becoming personalized and conflated into ideas of imposter syndrome.

L. Michelle's prescriptive insights, coaching and advice to double and triple down on the positive emotion is not only effective but essential to moving the needle toward getting more women of color into senior executive leadership and the C-Suite. She also layers on tenets of neuroscience that are particularly effective when coupled with positive emotion. Engaging what we know about how the brain learns and functions is crucial because the work of mindset shifting is tantamount to behavior change. The brain must unlearn certain cultural, generational and societal paradigms for these leaders to navigate corporate spaces that seem to work in a concerted way against their aspirations.

L. Michelle engages concepts like the progress loop, mindful listening, inattentional blindness, radical focus and more, but through a culturally nuanced lens, which is unique, provocative, relatable and most importantly, immediately applicable.

When I approached L. Michelle about penning the foreword in her next work, I was excited about how she would move this crucial narrative forward. You are going to hear more of her personal career anecdotes, her victories and her failures. You will hear from more extraordinary Black women C-Suite leaders who are a part of her tribe, and you will also hear from industry experts who are in the trenches each day working with women of color to crack the code to C-Suite access. What I really love about this book is the idea that coaching can get the reader further faster because we know in psychology that intrinsic motivation accomplishes this quicker than any other kind of motivation as it is grounded in one's passions, which are informed by personal values. That is the fuel anyone needs to go further faster, and the results are far more sustainable.

So, be certain to answer the coaching questions at the end of each chapter. And find ways to integrate the positive emotion strategies and affirmations that L. Michelle prescribes, especially for getting to the C-Suite. She is right: Black women aren't happy in corporate, and it is equally true that happy people are successful people. Allow this book to help you "find your happy." I can't wait to see how many lives are changed and how many more women of color realize their dreams to be C-Suite leaders as a result of this book.

Dr. Jeff Gardere, America's Psychologist

INTRODUCTION

What do you deserve?

Have you ever considered it? Often, we think about what we deserve when someone else raises the topic or tells us what we don't deserve. But for a moment, simply stop and ask yourself, "What do I *really* deserve?" Do you know?

The current state of our country may cause you to consider the question now more than ever. As of 2023, some have ventured to say that we are in a "post-pandemic" world. However, new cases and strains of COVID-19 are being reported every day. Some of us have had three and four rounds of jabs and boosters. By July 5, 2021, about 67% of U.S. citizens had received at least one dose of a COVID-19 vaccine, and companies were beginning to request workers come back into the office. But these people can't unsee what they saw. Life changed drastically during the lockdown, and this incredible time of change has caused many people to rethink their lives, their futures and the way they work. We are literally sitting in the very lap of change and the way we view life has shifted.

Some people made a distinct decision to opt out of work, leaving the job market. Women led the way. Some decided to start businesses. Others demanded that they continue to work from home or moved across the country in the new remote work environment because employers were not necessarily concerned with their employee's location at the time as long as they logged in each morning. Some fell in love. Others started families during the pandemic. Now more than ever, many of the people I've described are considering what they want, what they need and what they deserve. And Black women are definitely in this state of mind.

Some of my clients who are Black professional women love the idea of being "camera off" on all WebEx or Zoom calls for a couple of days each week, as they worked from home so didn't have to face people at work who clearly didn't like them or made their work lives hell. It's one clear sign that this digital economy is still fractured and the cultural context remains broken. It can be argued that the leadership void is less empty. We have a new President and a Vice President who is a woman of color. It is a major and historic milestone for our country. Things are looking up for the health crisis, but the tech industry has taken a hit with thousands of layoffs, and we've even witnessed a couple of small banks fold. War is still happening in Ukraine, and U.S. relationships with Russia and China remain strained and tense. Black people dying at the hands of police is still very much an issue.

In the summer of 2021, we saw some accountability in the wake of the murder of George Floyd, with former officer Derek Chauvin convicted and sentenced on various counts. However, earlier that spring, many were dumbfounded at how Breonna Taylor's killers were still at liberty. That was the day that I opened free emergency group coaching to any professional Black woman who wanted to join. They were all sitting behind their computers at home, aware of the decision not to charge the police officers who shot Breonna, but these women were still expected to work as if nothing had happened. It was time to emote, and sadly, these women couldn't find the space to do it, even in their homes, because work, and in some cases, online school, had invaded it. Hate crimes against Asian Americans spiked as well in the midst of pandemic racism, so the Black community wasn't the only one hurting.

Companies published their black tiles on Instagram and made their pledges of financial and programmatic support to the Black Community after George Floyd was killed, and a year later, the media echoed the question, "Where are the results?" High-performing Black professionals told me they were "All programmed out" and asked, "Is this really what we deserved?"

Knowing what you deserve takes time and reflection.

I remember the months leading up to the fall of 1989. The spring before, I had graduated from a small private school. I had stacks of brochures for schools I'd dreamed of attending but had only filled out one application. It was for the small private college that my sister attended, only about 20 miles from the house where I grew up. I really didn't want to go there, but my parents pretty much told me that this is what I would do. In fact, if you took Kiest Boulevard 25 minutes southwest of our home, you didn't have to make one turn, right or left, to arrive at the campus of the tiny Baptist college. Ultimately, I wouldn't attend there, even after applying and being awarded a full-ride scholarship that was snatched from me the minute I showed up to campus with all my blackness to register. Apparently, I looked white on paper.

That was close.

Within days, I'd find myself in the car with my mother, pointed west on Interstate 30. We were headed to what would become my alma mater, Texas Christian University, about a 45-minute drive from my house, but the tuition was astronomical—at least for my working-class parents. But this is what they wanted. I really didn't know anything about the school, but I was glad that it was a little further away...a little. They wanted me to get a good, solid education and my teaching certificate a short distance from home. It wasn't what I wanted, but when you're not paying, there's not much you can do or say about it.

As a result of not considering my dreams, I never once considered what I deserved. I don't even believe that dreaming was something my parents encouraged while I was growing up, so how could I ever ponder what I might deserve? They came from previous generations where survival was about all there was to think about. Who had the time, money or privilege to dream? I reflect on that time in my life today, many, many years later. Considering my own achievements, what might have happened if I had actually applied to Howard or Fisk? What if I had been accepted into Harvard? How much more excellent might I be? Might I have even dated and married a better life partner as a result? While I don't like to spend much time doing the "shoulda, coulda, woulda's," and clearly this was out of my control, it is human and understandable to wonder. Did I deserve to go to those schools? Did I deserve the resulting life? How much further along might I be than I am today? I was in my late teens then, but as adults, how often have we allowed others to dictate what we deserve?

When was the last time you allowed yourself to dream? What *do you* deserve? What is standing in the way of it?

Society has already decided what you deserve.

Let's take it one step further: have you ever considered what you might just be entitled to? Society says that a sense of entitlement isn't derived from a sense of goodness or the idea that you have worked hard for something. But that notion only applies to people who have privilege. They believe they are owed something and don't have to do anything to merit that something.

The fear of being accused of having a sense of entitlement also makes considering what one deserves a challenge for Black women and other women of color because it implies that we should only speak from a position of need. This also places us in a position of subservience once again. There's no winning in a losing stance.

Sometimes our families and community inadvertently or blatantly dictate what Black women deserve. Our gender can sideline us even in the Black family. Historically, as daughters, sisters, mothers and aunts, we've been told what we should do and how we should act, or at least there were expectations placed upon us. That's very different from the expectations applied to sons, brothers, uncles and fathers.

Culturally, Black women deal with the weight of expectations from their families and, historically, the Church. Often, the patriarchal expectations of denying oneself for the institution of marriage and family are noble, based on the traditional notion that even if you marry a jerk, it's better that there's a man around.

If you do marry, the interest of everyone in your family comes before yours, lest you be considered selfish. If, for some reason, you do not marry or have children, or even if you divorce or never marry but have a child, somehow you don't have room or a right to dream beyond the marriage construct. I have Black women clients who have been thrust into the responsibility of caring for aging parents, other elders and grandparents. They're required to put their entire lives on hold because they are the only sibling who is single with a great career. After all, according to family members, what else are they supposed to be doing? They don't have families themselves. Their families guilt them when these women try to set boundaries by deciding not to sacrifice their peace or careers for something their siblings could take on or, at the very least, share. But because their siblings have families, or merely because they are men, they are not faced with the same expectations to pack up and move to another part of the country or drive for miles on weekends or personally pay thousands for care and support to care for a family member or even take them into their own homes. How can you dream or even know what you deserve if your family and community tell you that your one role in life is to support everyone else above yourself?

It is perpetuated in dating by men who discount a woman's success and leadership aspirations and see them as a liability and not an asset. Many of these men find their primary value in their careers and their ability to make money. When they meet women who place a similar premium on their careers there is instant conflict. These men expect their dreams to be centered above the woman's and resent them being equally yoked in this way. Heaven forbid a woman make more money, have a better title, career or even a better car. Love is simply stamped out with pure resentment in these situations.

Conversely, if you happen to have the benefit and true blessing of having a partner, family, community or even tribe that does not buy into centering maleness at all costs and instead tells you that you deserve everything because you have value, you still may walk into a world and a workplace that is built to center white maleness.

So, the ultimate message to Black women is that they are undeserving. They experience a consistent push-pull between negative messages in the world and workplace and the positive messages from their tribe if they have one. Knowing that you are deserving can be challenging, depending on what message you received last or most often. As for those women who feel they have no source to re-enforce their worth because they lack access to advocates, sponsors or mentors in corporate America, the question is how do you realize you actually do deserve the extraordinary perks and opportunities that executive leadership can offer?

In my research for *Yes Please*, I surveyed 100 Black women professionals. An overwhelming 90% of those responding agreed that they find it to be a challenge to be a Black woman in corporate America. Even more agreed that either their race or their race and gender were the primary obstacle standing in the way of their day-to-day efforts to rise in leadership, with 55% of them saying that they had no access to sponsors. Sponsors not only let you know that you are deserving, but they also step up for you and advocate for the positions they believe you deserve. No wonder many Black women and women of color have difficulty wrapping their heads around what they deserve or are entitled to. They lack access to the very group that can reinforce and *act* on the fact that Black women are due a seat at the most important decision-making tables in business.

What we deserve as humans, but not everyone receives.

According to the website "Good Therapy," being deserving means "Having an expectation of goodness in your life. It is the goodness of people, relationships and situations that we all want and deserve in our lifetime."

We can agree that we all deserve

- » a safe place to live and work
- » relationships and people who love us
- » colleagues and employers who respect and support us

Often, the latter is more elusive for Black women and other women of color. So, when I write that high-performing women of color need to shift their mindset to realize their own entitlement, it means that they should receive the same rewards and recognition that anyone would, in exchange for an equal amount of good work and excellence that it typically takes to achieve these wonderful things.

We don't live in a society where that is the case. High-performing professional Black women and other women of color have been taught and have experienced that working 120% may get you invited into a room, but it may not get you to the place where real decisions are made. So, to understand that she is deserving or entitled to the rewards of C-Suite leadership requires her to be the Simone Biles of mental gymnastics. Imagine living and working in a society that teaches you that you are worthless. Instead, we must definitely tell ourselves that we are indeed worthy and have others who care and are invested in us share that thought consistently and often.

When was the last time you felt worthy or deserving? Now ask yourself, why not at work? And why not for my executive leadership aspirations?

Dr. Miki Kashtan suggests in *Psychology Today* that we take the idea of deserving to another level with our language, since the word itself implies that you have a right to something. She's correct. However, having the right to something implies that we should make demands. Of course, in some cases, demanding what you want or should have may not be popular, but it may be a necessity. More often than not, engaging more honey will move you forward faster than purely unleashing the vinegar. She suggests that we move to a language that is more needs-based. The reality is that what Black women and other women of color are looking for when it comes to more opportunities in executive leadership is definitely a need. Currently, there are only two Black women at the helm of Fortune 500 companies, up a whopping two CEOs since I released the *No Thanks* books, where I chronicled the retirement of Ursula Burns from Xerox in 2016. There is definitely a need. Black women make up just 7.4% of all executive positions in Fortune 500 companies, according to Catalyst. Black women *need* to be represented. Black women have a need and desire to lead in significant ways, according to the 2021 Black Women in Corporate America report from Leanin.org. So, when we move to needs-based language in our pursuit of what we want, we connect better with others, Kashtan suggests.

> *"...the language of needs more easily lends itself to continuing to see the humanity of the person or people whose actions we aim to change through struggle. This changes the nature of the struggle, the form of the fight. Nonviolence has as one of its prerequisites the commitment to love no matter what. We can more easily love our opponent when we can see*

and connect with their human needs than when we see them only through the effect that their choices have on us, and therefore subtly or not so subtly believe they deserve some punishment for their actions. Even when we oppose people's choices, even when we make it impossible for them to continue what they are doing through massive nonviolent resistance, we can, and have been known to do so while seeing their humanity with love."

It takes honey and vinegar to get us to the C-Suite.

I believe that in the case of the Black woman's quest for executive leadership, the approach is the language of deserving *and* need. We have to spike our honey with a touch of vinegar. I also believe that we need to take a cue from our more privileged counterparts as they tend to display their sense of entitlement subtly and boldly with much more ease and frequency. My sisters have been held down for so long. We have been conditioned to believe that humility wins in a corporate culture that is ultimately cut-throat and born from a capitalistic society that was built on the ideas of imperialism, colonization and manifest destiny. Our generation-over-generation community-first mentality leaves us in a mindset that doesn't necessarily position us well for winning in "the American way."

Black women need to over-rotate to begin to compensate for the time lost. They need to exchange the false sense of humility that they've been taught to emulate [instead of properly merchandising themselves and their work or building a personal brand] for a visible and unapologetic strength.

What stops many Black women from considering their deservedness deeply is that they believe they may slip into a sense of entitlement in the process. That is the idea that you deserve a favor simply because you exist. It is the attitude that says that you are owed something. In fact, *WebMD* discussed the entitlement mentality in a 2017 article and linked it to a narcissistic personality disorder. Not to say that everyone who feels entitled has been clinically diagnosed, but that their attitudes reflect the tendency to be narcissistic. The article is the first that I've come across that even implicitly links privilege to narcissism, understanding that people who are privileged exercise a sense of entitlement.

"People with an entitlement mentality often see themselves as superior to others. It's no surprise that this way of thinking affects interpersonal relationships."

Entitlement has a negative connotation. So does privilege. So why is it fine for me to suggest that marginalized people take on some aspects of these traits? It's because people who are othered, marginalized and otherwise not centered are required to make great leaps in their minds and hearts about whether they are deserving. That's because society is set to *ensure* that they are positioned as not so. The un-centered are required to wage an internal war against the constant negativity, spoken or unspoken. That negative energy is literally airborne. It seeps into the pores. It surrounds and discourages on a consistent basis.

Taking a dose of entitlement for the marginalized is like good medicine. It allows us a glimpse of what it is like to walk into a room with authority simply because one exists. Like an overdrawn bank account thirsts for a little extra cash to not only satisfy the overdraft but supply some relief from the negative balance, so is the heart, mind and soul of those who are othered. This is exactly the reason why affirming that someone owes you is more than correct. Black women begin and oftentimes end their careers at a deficit in achievement, affirmation and compensation.

Over-credentialed, high-performing Black women and other women of color who are excellent are entitled to the C-Suite, and we should walk tall in that affirmation, claiming it every day, knowing that subconsciously others are programmed to believe that we are not, and work to ensure that we cannot obtain that position. With the country's less than stellar track record on race heralding all the way back to 1619, many argue that someone *indeed* owes Black Americans. They call it reparations. In this case, I believe Black women professionals are due because we understand that doing twice the work may only get you invited to the party. It doesn't necessarily mean you'll be asked to dance.

My Sister, when you assume your position of visible strength, think of a lioness poised to fight when necessary yet sitting in her regal stance. This is the posture that is merited to get us where we need and deserve to go, and dare I say, where we are entitled to go…to the C-Suite. It's a journey that isn't for the faint of heart but for the ones with cunning and fighter instincts.

This book will lean heavily on the science of positive emotion, with each chapter beginning with a positive affirmation and concluding with coaching. Consider it as much a guide as an executive coaching tool with tenets of neuroscience and positive psychology at its core.

Are you ready to do what it takes to get what you deserve and what you are entitled to?

This is your signal to say, *Yes Please!*

1 GUIDING PRINCIPLE

YOU MUST BE HAPPY TO DO THIS, SIS

The year was 2009. I'd received an offer to become a Senior Vice President at a global agency, and that offer included everything I had asked for. It definitely brought a smile to my face, but it was a temporary one. I was battling demons at home. I tried to savor the moment. After all, this position wasn't a heavy lift to secure. My tribe had jumped into action.

As I was contemplating the closure of my own boutique agency, I simply picked up the phone or shot notes to the heads of the local offices of global agencies. Within short order, I found myself in interviews with several high-ranking officers at this one firm. Just weeks later, the offer arrived and I accepted it without any doubt. It was exactly what I believed I deserved. I even brought with me two small accounts from my boutique agency and left two employees behind at my Dallas-based headquarters to close things out through the end of the year. It was an accomplishment to be in this position, to say the least. But then I heard these words at home: "You make entirely too much money." The man I was married to at the time was looking at some documents that we were sending off before moving. There was no lift in his voice to show that he was joking with me. He was dead serious. It was a sign of resentment, and that raw emotion was living with me under my own roof.

Three-week-long "business trips" and other indiscretions had become the norm, but on the heels of a miscarriage the year before there was one positive glimmer that kept me hoping things might smooth out for me. I was thrilled to learn that my rainbow baby was on her way, but it was not news that I wanted to share too early with anyone outside of my immediate family since I'd previously lost a baby within the first ten weeks.

Operating at your greatest in a high-ranking position is tough when you aren't happy mentally, spiritually or even physically at home or at work. I had morning sickness in the morning, noon *and* night. I was commuting at least 90 minutes to work each morning in stressful traffic and dealing with strife at home. In hindsight, I know that my unhappiness was obvious and it was clear in how I showed up, no matter how I tried to disguise it. In addition, the new workplace was not the warmest environment. It was pretty ruthless and petty.

I had a Karen-type client whose only mission was to undermine me by meeting with my team without my knowledge and gossiping about whether I might be pregnant and needing to go on leave. She also complained that I was "too cool" when I successfully handled minor issues and crisis management. She said she wanted to see me "sweat" a little more. With more than 20 years under my belt and no extreme crisis at hand, there wasn't anything to sweat about. She also wanted me to be more subservient and tactical than consultative, and all my talk of strategy was falling on deaf and far more junior ears than my own. The worst part of all: she was determined to trot out the news of my pregnancy to my team and other clients before I was ready to make the announcement. She was the quintessential microaggressive bully. Syrupy sweet to my face but always wielding a dagger when I wasn't around.

The bullying was so bad that I went to Human Resources to report the behavior, but to no avail. It was very disappointing, considering the HR professional was not only Black like me but a church member. To this day, I still don't understand why this particular HR person expects me to be happy to see her in the pews when we happen to bump into each other. I suppose my blank stare isn't enough for her to get it. She was a part of the hatchet job that would eventually culminate with my departure. I even had colleagues who were working overtime to take over my main account and further poison the client against me. I had managed to grow this account by 50% in less than three months despite my challenges, personal and professional, but they waited until I was on family leave to snatch the account from beneath me.

All this was more than exhausting. So when it was time to return to work after having the baby, I knew that either I would be quitting them or they would be quitting me. It was probably the one thing on which my then husband and I saw eye-to-eye. It was time for me to go.

In a big agency, if you don't have the billable hours to support your existence, they can lay you off with no explanation other than there isn't enough work to support your position. So after signing a few documents, I was off with my lump sum. Not even three months after leaving that position, with my baby girl barely six months old, I was recruited for a role at a big company. I was moving about in a dense fog, not even able to see that I would be facing divorce less than 90 days later, and I had not even accrued time off to deal with it.

These were the toughest times of my life. In retrospect, the divorce and custody proceedings took much less time than most. But while I was in it, it seemed like forever. These were some of the darkest days of my life. Only two weeks after all was final, I would find myself on a plane headed to New York. One of my agency teams and I were headed to an awards ceremony to ultimately claim three trophies. I definitely deserved this recognition, and it was proof positive that the people I worked for before weren't interested in my success. Yet here I was at a Fortune 10, taking home awards after a little over a year in the role, with most of that time spent in divorce proceedings and transitioning to an official role as Mom-in-Chief.

It was then that I thought to myself, "Imagine what I could have done if I were happy." A few weeks later, I would make that declaration to one of my bosses on the walk back from lunch:

"Thank you for supporting me through such a rough time, and I promise you, when I come out of this fog, I will perform in ways that you never knew that I could."

I remember her eyes widening in response. Then she said, "Well, that would be amazing after bringing that Silver Anvil home. I can't imagine how much better you could be."

Fast forward seven years, and while I worked frantically to do my hair and makeup before going on stage to speak at a large conference, one of forty engagements that year, I was listening in on my executive coaching certification courses, and there it was – research in applied positive psychology that said something so crucial: *Happy people are successful people.* The fact is that even if you are unhappy and manage a few wins, it is not sustainable. So, you must do the work to *get happy* and learn how to sustain it because your happiness is *completely* up to you.

I believe that being happy is the best state to be in to truly consider what you deserve. It is safe to say that my journey to happy began by shedding a toxic marriage and work environment to dive headfirst into therapy that chipped away at all the "whys" so that I could heal, protect my happiness, my peace, be the best mother to my daughter and sustain it all. Life is challenging enough without adding in workplace drama. But what if we could be intentional about securing happiness in all aspects of our lives?

Black women in the corporate workplace are not happy.

How will Black women succeed if they are rarely happy at work? In my story, those glimmers of happiness were indeed episodic. I needed to carry my own source of happiness with me. I was reminded constantly of the old gospel tune that says, "This joy that I have you didn't give, can't take it away." That line is so true, but only if you have a keen awareness of where your happiness comes from. Science has shown us that people who are truly happy rely on their values to uncover and sustain their contentment. My values are faith, family and freedom. They became my North Star in life as I realized them between 2016-2019.

Just think: what if I had the privilege to walk into that officer role at that challenging agency and face microaggressive behavior and only had to deal with the drama at home? Chances are I would have been able to compartmentalize the strife and be more mentally prepared to lead and win. I may have been in a better position to face what was looming in the hallways and in the offices next to my own. How do I know this? I filed for divorce only two months after joining the big company, which by comparison, had a much better workplace culture. I had a chain of supportive bosses and clients in the business units and agency teams that were ready and able to support my goals.

That support at work certainly did help. And instead of that support being episodic, the microaggressions were. That is a switch for most of us. So, despite my circumstances at home, I had a clear shot at succeeding and soaring. Unfortunately, Black women and other women of color don't often get the luxury of being happy at work. It became even more clear to me when I surveyed 100 professional Black women about their experiences in corporate America.

Black women leaders really aren't happy about their daily lives in some of the most elite workplaces. Joy was not a word that a majority of respondents used in the survey to describe their experiences in the corporate workplace. In fact, 90% described being a Black woman in the corporate world as a "challenge," with 45% of respondents calling their experience stressful or saying they are ready to completely try something new. Another 43% described their experience as "Meh."

This is a problem. How can Black women reach their rockstar leadership aspirations if they aren't happy? Compounded by the bias, the lack of access to sponsors, mentors and the perks that executive leadership provides, like access to executive coaches and opportunities to grow generational wealth, many Black women find themselves settling in a holding pattern at 10,000 feet before they are ever released to soar to the heights to which they actually aspire.

The 2020 State of Black Women in Corporate America report from Leanin.org found that Black women are substantially more likely than white women, and just as likely as white men, to say they are interested in becoming top executives. These are the eagles, not everyone. They are the high-performing, high-potential, professional Black women. But somewhere along the way, 10, 15 or even 20 years into their careers, they've forgotten or pressed down those aspirations. What do Black women need to do to get to their happy in order to thrive in an exclusive corporate workplace? What are the secrets that no one talks about when it comes to climbing into top leadership? How are some of the most successful women guarding their happiness and their peace?

One of the secrets that most top CEOs agree with is the importance of remaining positive and increasing your positive emotions as much as possible. It's much easier to be positive if you are happy, but the science of happiness actually highlights the fact that being positive can create that great outlook that leads to more happiness. According to ScienceOfPeople.com, citing as its source many of the classic studies from applied positive psychology, the most successful CEOs have found the following habits helpful in keeping a positive attitude and boosting happiness:

- » finding your positive affirmation
- » surrounding yourself with truly positive, uplifting people
- » doing daily exercise
- » staying off social media and doing a digital detox
- » practicing confident body language
- » performing a random act of kindness
- » telling yourself three things you're grateful for in the morning
- » finding time for daily meditation
- » starting a gratitude journal
- » replacing negative reading with positive books

These are all great. Most of the white male CEOs swear by them, and science supports the fact that they work. But what science is out there to support Black women and women of color who have even more obstacles stacked on top of the typical demands on a C-Suite executive? Unfortunately, it is not there. Science doesn't center Black women either, so there is a gap in the data from a cultural perspective.

Fortunately, however, there is data that shows that Black women indeed face more challenges than white male leaders, and to many extents, their white female counterparts or even other men and women of color, while they may have their own nuanced battles. So I went on a quest to find out what Black women who have made it to the officer level do to cultivate and keep their own happiness when the obstacles are steeper for them than most. While I had them, I also asked about the things that no one told them before they arrived at their posts and the things that they wished they'd known before they started their journeys. I also spoke with some experts in the space. We covered all sorts of topics, from navigating being the only one in the room to the tips no one bothers to share that can positively affect your ability to produce generational wealth. I also continue to share vignettes from my own experience.

Sis, the road that you have chosen is not an easy one. What I will share in the pages to come may surprise you, but if you are armed with the right knowledge, you can reach the C-Suite as well and do so with a genuine smile on your face.

2 AFFIRMATION #1

"I AM LIKABLE AND BRING VALUE TO ANY SPACE"

Secret: It isn't simply who you know, it's who likes you and the value you bring

O nce again, I found myself sitting in the office of a high-ranking officer. This time, my job was to secure a mandate for the implementation of a concept I created that would save the company money and mitigate risks to its reputation and, therefore, its bottom line. There was also an opportunity to increase profit because it would broaden the reach of our messages. Meeting in his office had become at least a quarterly happening since he moved to the C-Suite so I wasn't uncomfortable there. And I felt that if I could sell this plan, it could have a long-lasting impact on my career and upward trajectory.

I made it to the first slide, a chart that shared some key data about the insight that drove the entire concept. Then, he stopped me, examined it, asked a couple of questions, and said, "You know, I want you to share this with both of my VPs in a meeting that I will arrange because I need both of them on board and working with their teams."

This was a win. I hadn't even completed my presentation, and he was already granting his mandate. So I agreed and clicked on the next slide. Before I could continue, he asked me a question that I considered a bit off-topic and a wee bit awkward: "Do you want my job?" he asked.

I was stunned. What in the world?

"I'm not sure I follow," I said.

"Just what I said. Do you want my job?" he repeated. There was a long, pregnant pause. Was this a trick question? Where was this going? I hesitated again.

"The CEO and I look across the business to identify successors, people who are about at your career stage. You can outthink everyone on that floor, and when you work on projects, you grow them. You find the money and they just get bigger and bigger. And so I'm asking you, do you want my job?"

At this point, my eyes were wide open, but what he said did indeed compute. "I see. So we are having *that* conversation," I said,

"Well, in that case..." I said slowly. "I'd love to have your boss' job." His eyes widened, "Now, we're talking! That's good to know."

Then the conversation turned to more personal data points, like where I attended church, more about my family and some things about my daughter. Someone had finally broached one of those conversations that you only hear about, the coveted succession conversation. I was outdone. I wasn't ready, but I was. I was prepared, but I didn't think it would happen so soon or like this.

My biggest takeaway from the incident was more about the conversation that ensued after the big question, where he was interested in my dad's table tennis game and other subjects like that. This was a conversation about "likability." Apparently, I'd cleared the "Can she do the job and can she lead?" hurdle.

This is the first time I've shared this conversation in a broad way. I didn't even share it with a sponsor. I shared it with a mentor. I shared it with a close tribe member and confidant, but it's one you keep very close to your vest as it also makes you an enemy of some key players. That part is something I was naive about.

DE&I and leadership development expert Dr. Christopher Butts told me that these kinds of conversations are the ones that no one really talks about but that Black women can indeed prepare for.

"They're the conversations that don't show up on the paperwork but they're the conversations that add to the story that they're making up about you as they review your credentials, and being prepared for those conversations is challenging because it goes back to that balancing act," Butts said. "How professional do I present myself, and how personable do I present myself? And how much personal information do I share? Because nine times out of ten [and it sounds horrible, but the research backs it up], people hire other people that are like them. So if you know, and it's funny if you know, information on the person that you're getting ready to go meet with, it really makes it easier for you to spark some sort of relationship, some sort of connection. Oh, we went to school in the South together. Or we both went to an HBCU. Or you know, I know you played tennis."

Early in my career, my Baby Boomer mentors shared with me that it was more important to be respected than to be liked. I found out that respect was good, but the premium was on likability. This was new, and it presents a different set of considerations for the doubly disadvantaged. If Black women and other women of color are not centered, how in the world do we become likable in an environment which was not built in our favor?

In fact, the idea that my father was a table tennis champion did indeed come up, and it was a point of connection between this particular officer and myself.

Let's face it, as Black women in professional settings, being liked is generally unexpected, and being unliked is probably the norm. Not only that, but it can be the source of plenty of unhappiness. In this instance, I was blessed to have a C-Suite leader who was progressive and prone to see talent before much else. When you have leaders like this, these conversations will happen more often than not. It was the middle managers who would ultimately pose the most friction to my forward motion, and there was at least one other C- Suite member who felt it was her duty to shut down my progress. It was motivated by her need to build a platform for herself. She felt I had too much external and internal influence with her C-Suite rival, the same leader who asked me the succession questions.

Let's be clear: everyone won't like you, and being liked isn't the goal. The goal is *likability*. There is a difference, and who finds you likable matters. Those people must be the ones in positions to ask questions like "Do you want my job?" That should be a relief to hear for most Black women with top leadership aspirations because the structure of corporate America was built to favor people who are not us.

Some of them will never like you, especially if you get in their way.

It is tough to get everyone to like working with you even if you aren't in the margins, and ultimately, it is impossible no matter who you are. This kind of likability is much more the result of a perfect storm of people in high places who are willing to not only advocate but fight for you and influence others to consider liking you too. It's important to know that your happiness cannot depend on whether you have likability or not. Sis, you need to like yourself first. Far too often, we allow how everyone else feels about us to be a factor in our self-assurance and esteem.

If you are wondering how I went from having a successful conversation with a C-Suite leader to, less than two years later, sitting across from that same officer discussing how he and his peers wanted to keep me at that company after receiving a surplus notice, I can tell you why succinctly: I am a high-performing Black woman. My story is the reflection of so many other women of color in an array of industries and companies, and their stories are all the same. You can only soar for a few years or so before someone decides to undermine or remove you, and not all those people have to be white or male. This particular officer's rival wanted me out of the spotlight with regard to speaking about the company's commitment to diversity and inclusion. Later, she would take over the department along with another officer who just didn't understand what my team did with diversity and inclusion anyway. And that is when I noticed my time at work was pretty miserable, and my upward trajectory stalled. My primary sponsor announced her retirement the previous summer, shocking everyone. My sponsorship had waned suddenly as a result. I became a target and, to a vocal minority, pretty unlikable. They didn't know what or why I was doing the work I was doing. Simply doing my job became a threat and counter to the status quo. Shining became a detriment.

This is the primary reason why your happiness cannot be rooted in what others think of you at work or, for that matter, anywhere else. Their opinions can change faster than an org chart in a shifting business. Just ask the author, speaker, founder and CEO of Cultural Solutions Group, Dorinda Walker. Her reputation went from top producer to corporate menace when her personal brand took off in tandem with her career at a large insurance firm. She was on a rocket.

"A new CEO came on board who happened to be one of the people who advocated for me early on in my career. But there were a lot of organizational changes, and they decided to merge my department in with the brand advertising department," Walker said. "And quite honestly, the head of brand advertising, in my opinion, based on my experience, was biased towards Black women and especially towards me."

Walker believes the leader had it out for her because he couldn't take credit for her work.

"He felt some kind of way because I didn't work with him. So he wasn't getting the accolades I was getting. And when I say accolades, any award that an executive can get, I got it," Walker said. "So when I merged into his department, they took away my staff. They took away my budget, gave me a new title. But basically, I felt like my talent wasn't being utilized in a way that was going to fulfill me."

So Walker left her healthy six-figure role and started her own consultancy. Her story isn't new. As I coach Black women in the Fortune 100 I hear the same story from high-performing Black women leaders. The only thing that changes is their names and titles. However, the result is the same. This putting of us in our places, this quiet firing, this demotion without calling it that, strips us of our joy. It crushes our happiness.

"And the realization came to me because I was coming to work miserable, not liking what I was doing, and I felt like I was starting over. And I was going into rooms having to educate a room full of non-people of color about why culture and diversity matters," she said. "And I felt like I was doing that my whole career. I don't want to start over. So one day, I pulled up in the garage, and I didn't want to go in. I didn't want to go into the building."

The naysayers begin to tarnish your reputation and drop seeds that feed the negative tropes. "She's hard to work with." Translation: "She isn't accepting our efforts to shut her down." Or, despite your executive level status: "I need her to be tactical, prescriptive and roll up her sleeves. She keeps giving us strategy and delegating." They didn't care enough to ask the officer who asked me to do that work about my assignment. Others refused to take a meeting with me on topics where I was the sole subject matter expert. They didn't look into why I was winning awards, and they didn't care. They just wanted everything I was doing to stop because it annoyed them and the leader who tweeted to her limited social media following that she was an "inclusion warrior." Later, she would turn the bulk of the department into her personal news bureau, moving budget from that same department, nearly destroying it, so that the money would benefit her original core team.

Likability aside, your happiness must come from within. In fact, you must have enough happiness in the love bank to offset the miserable feelings that come for you in situations like these so that you don't experience an overdraft.

Managing your likability as a Black woman is like Olympic-caliber gymnastics.

Is it possible to be likable and be a Black woman in a corporate environment all at once? The answer is a qualified yes; you can likely have some success at it if you can get comfortable with the fact that likability, in our case,

- » isn't an always-on, 24-7, 360-degree arrangement,
- » that it always has an expiration date,
- » and that it is never guaranteed.

However, imagine that you need to have the timing, agility and sheer magical ability of a Simone Biles to navigate it. [And even she couldn't catch a break, being punished for her abilities which were far superior to her competitors.] One day, you'll need to dominate on the balance beam. On another day, you'll need to do three consecutive fulls in your floor exercise. But then you'll need to be prepared to hear that the judges believe that you're doing too much, and they will disqualify your moves because no one else can do them but you. You may even find yourself learning to accept the fact that those same judges and fans are tired of seeing you win, believing that while you may be the best and *the beast* at what you do, it's time that you just stepped aside and give someone else a turn at winning, as was asserted some years ago about tennis stars Venus and Serena Williams. It is the same sentiment that Tiger Woods endured at some point in his career. But as we can see, his comeback game, like the others I've mentioned, is strong. This is the burden of resilience that high-performing Black leaders bear. That resilience comes at a high and unfair cost, but it grants beast mode to the best of us.

They will inevitably say that you are doing too much. They will resent your shining. Between the time of the succession conversation and the surplus conversation with that same officer, I learned that my speaking on platforms at the request of external business organizations and conferences had been questioned by my colleagues to their bosses. No one bothered to establish that I had been asked by my superiors to continue to speak as much as I could because it was "good for business." Neither were they aware that although there was a freeze on the travel budget for my department, my flights and hotels were being paid for by the external organizations that were inviting me. Some decided that I was simply breaking the rules, believing someone was just allowing me to go unchecked. They were even tracking my comings and goings on social media.

These speaking engagements were often linked to the awards for the work that my teams were doing. Next, I would learn that someone didn't like that I used the word "teams" in those write-ups about the awards. They wanted me to take the "s" off when I had multiple agency teams and an internal team handling up to nine different marketing segments under my direction. The awards we were receiving were for the concept that I shared in that meeting with the officer with whom the succession conversation occurred. We wouldn't even activate it for another six months, at which point I would have 80 people across three marketing organizations directed by their VPs and other superiors as part of what was essentially a center of excellence on that topic.

Likability for Black women can be directly proportionate to the power and influence she does or does not wield.

It was interesting to see the counter-narrative that developed on my floor as all of this was going on. While my growing influence was affecting decisions in every room where marketing decisions were made, I watched as a handful of other Black women were being elevated in areas that were much less meaningful. At corporate events, there were at least three Black women who were less known for their work and more known for their ability to entertain during and after work hours and at internal events. But these women contributed very little to the actual strategic vision or execution of the work of the department. Instead, they were the first to raise their hands to bring the banana pudding to the potluck or even organize the next mandatory fun event. The ones who did make notable contributions were the quiet workhorses, and they were diminished. It seemed years would pass before any of the ones doing the real work were considered for promotions, and that was as long as they stayed quiet with their heads down and didn't kick up dust.

The likability that counts comes from the eagles.

I've concluded that complete likability across an enterprise might just be impossible for Black women and other women of color, so we must aim for the likability that counts. Don't get me wrong, it wasn't lost on me that I had obtained not only the respect but the hearts and minds of many, many people across that mammoth company, some that I didn't even know. I joke to this day that while there were likely four people who tried to undermine me, that would mean I considered the thousands of others to be pretty cool colleagues. To this day, I have people from that company whom I never met in person who message me to tell me that they heard me speak or have been following me on Linkedin since my early days there. At all-company events, I would be tracked down to take selfies with employees I had no idea knew me, and I had clients in other business units who spoke loudly and proudly about my work and my impact. But, Sis, it really only takes a handful of monkeys to tilt the barrel and sometimes overturn it, and it may surprise you who is willing to do the dirty work. So you mustn't aim for broad likability. The corporate environment wasn't built with you in mind. You must aim for *strategic* likability.

In *No Thanks: 7 Ways to Say I'll Just Include Myself*, I shared the analogy of the chickens and the eagles as well as the chickens in eagles' outfits. Eagles see other eagles and, for the most part, will understand you and support you in your efforts to be a transformational leader. Unfortunately, there are more chickens than eagles, and while some chickens will admire you and all your "eagleness," some will make it their life's work to tear you down because they just don't like you in the first place. However, when the right eagles believe in you, how and where you can soar is boundless.

Regrettably, many Black women and women of color think of the limits before they consider what soaring even looks or feels like. In short, we trade our ability to dream for what we believe it looks like when the chickens begin their clucking. I've asked a few clients when we first engaged what they want to be doing in two years. The silence is deafening. While they comb their minds, they begin to think about what can't happen before they consider what they want. They think of the limitations of the head count on their teams or that their current boss won't retire for years. They consider the bounds of their current employer, and they don't even dare mention their personal lives. Because we've seen what has happened to so many of us in corporate spaces, we allow that to dictate our dreams. Do we even know how to dream anymore?

Write the big check, forget the boundaries, then cash it.

In conversation with the Chief Equity & Impact Officer of Omnicom, one of the youngest C-Suite executives in the global agency realm, and one of the only Black woman C-Suite executives in that space, Emily K. Graham told me that her breakthrough moment came when a mentor told her she wasn't dreaming big enough.

"They were too small, and they had too many boundaries. So, he advised me to think as if he had given me a blank check and to write the amount that I wanted," Graham said. "And once I wrote it, tear that check up and write it double. That is when I started getting into the realm of what I was worth. That conversation and counsel from him changed the way I viewed what I wanted and what value I brought."

Graham, who was named to PR Week's 2021 Top 40 Under 40 public relations leaders to watch list, secured the respect of her teams, who rave publicly about working with her, but she also won the likability wars by securing the mentorship and sponsorship of some of the most powerful people in the global agency realm. She credits that one conversation with moving her career forward by light years after it happened four years ago, more than 15 years into her journey as a standout communications leader. She was the first Chief Diversity & Inclusion Officer for Omnicom agency Fleishman-Hillard, but that would only mushroom the media coverage that began stacking up for her as one of the youngest senior leaders at the helm of some of the largest Fortune 500 accounts the agency had on its roster. So it took some brand-building to get her to her now, and the verdict remains the same for most Black women: when you receive that level of "shine," some will not like it, but you have to push forward anyway.

Look at her now!

Understand that the odds favoring the power of your voice will have a bigger payoff than any looming threat to silence you.

Lafern Kitt Batie is the founder and CEO of The Batie Group. She is also one of my mentor coaches. She has found that when working with Black women and other women of color who have senior leadership aspirations, they impose their own boundaries on how far they can climb by silencing their own voices at the most critical times.

"Your voice is the most powerful asset that you'll ever have," Batie said. "Sometimes, I've seen Black women and other women of color go into those spaces and be silent. And knowing that you can't afford to do that for so long, the best advice I ever received was...I need you to come out of the observation role, and I need you to get in the ring. They need to know your voice."

The kind of likability that propels you forward comes from being heard and seen when it matters most. Unfortunately, when the pandemic locked us down and banished many Black women leaders to their home offices, it became easier to go into "listen-only mode." The desire not to engage took over as the cultural context bore down on women of color. This included the George Floyd murder. The trial of the police officer who killed him. The hearing on Breonna Taylor which registered no charges against the police officers who gunned down the unarmed woman in her home. These headlines happened while the status quo continued: microaggressions can be virtual too. So many Black women with leadership aspirations did what anyone would do when they are tired of work and taxed by life in general, such as the day-to-day challenges at home that the pandemic presented: they turned off their cameras and stayed on mute as much as possible.

A 2021 Washington Post article called "Many Black women felt relieved to work from home, free from microaggressions; now they are asked to come back" revealed that, according to a Gallup survey, one of the primary reasons Black women are hesitant to return to the office is that they feel undervalued at work. The work-from-home culture that the pandemic fostered allowed Black women to create their own safe spaces and digital communities that enabled them to focus solely on work. They don't have to deal with the day-to-day microaggressions previously faced in the workplace or can easily avoid them. Perhaps the microaggressions were not even day-to-day, but they still felt real to many of my clients. Several of them found ways to mitigate the feelings, finding sanctuary with the technology that buffered them from the threats and still allowed them to lead.

Plan to speak up in meetings and make a schedule for how you engage.

For those of you who tend to hang back in meetings in person and never say a word, it's important to plan for engagement in online meetings, even as many workplaces welcome back a hybrid workforce. While it may be a bit impossible to plan what to say because others may say the same thing, it is not unreasonable to plan to engage with an insightful question on a topic that you know will arise. Try to make the question open-ended, something that will encourage conversation and position you as smart, thoughtful and engaged. This requires you to listen to the entire meeting.

As for being camera-off because constantly putting on "the face" may feel like a bit much during these times, many of my clients, most of them working mothers, have learned that proactively setting boundaries not only manages expectations but provides them with a much-needed respite when required. This maintains their psychological safety as well as preserves their happiness. Designate camera-off days instead of sporadically turning off your webcam. If everyone understands that on Fridays, for instance, you will not be seen, it manages expectations with no surprises.

Positive emotion is paramount to successfully navigating strategic likability.

Everyone won't like you, even if they smile in your face or look like you. So, there is a measure of resilience and grit that is mandatory that should undergird your mind and heart in order to move forward with confidence despite the haters. As I coach mid-to-high-ranking Black women executives and explore their experiences with self-doubt, I continue to discover that their battles with their inner critic typically originate with the thoughts and expressions that other people thrust upon them. This puts an entirely new spin on limiting beliefs, because that inner critic has her origins from external sources. Cognitive behavioral theory suggests that automatic negative thoughts (ANTs) can eat away at our motivation but can be countered with positive self-talk. Experts in applied positive psychology have uncovered ten positive emotions. However, they say you must summon at least three of them for every negative feeling in order to be happy. According to a recent article by Dr. Tom Muha,

> *"Numerous studies have affirmed that dipping below the 3:1 positive-negative threshold puts people into a state of languishing or suffering. Simply said, you're either feeling quiet desperation or despair."*

This seems to be where many Black women and women of color become mired in the toxicity of corporate America. They are not staying above the 3:1 positive emotion threshold. They may not be aware of the positive emotions they need to access in order to offset the negativity. They are simply becoming worn out, some of them even depressed, and they never make their executive leadership aspirations a reality because, frankly, they are emotionally spent.

In this day of internet coaches of every ilk, credentialed or otherwise, affirmations and mantras are thrown around like free candy. But these sayings are only as effective as their construction and the number of times that you say them to yourself. Neuroscience applications for affirmations stress repetition so that the brain's center of learning, the hippocampus, expands and grows. It isn't enough to put the statements on a sticky note and look at them once a day. Seeing, writing, saying and hearing them throughout the day is imperative – the more repetition, the better.

In fact, findings in neuroscience also reveal that adding proof and reason to the affirmation increases its effectiveness. Simply adding the word "because" after the affirmation and then articulating proof of that affirmation allows the brain to engage and believe the affirmation. For those suffering from chronic self-doubt, neuroscientists recommend beginning the affirmation with the proof, then inserting the "because" followed by the positive statement.

Here are examples of this tactic:

Adding reason to the affirmation:

I am excellent and likable because officers in the company call on me frequently for stretch assignments.

For self-doubters:

Officers in this company call on me frequently for stretch assignments because I am excellent and likable.

Think about it: if you feel that the room doesn't like you when you walk into it, and you continue going into that room, soon you will begin to question if you're simply unlikable. Repeated negative emotion has the same and sometimes a more powerful effect on our mind as positive emotion. In some cases, you may start to believe that you aren't likable. We need to triple down on our positive affirmations in order to combat the negative effects of these thoughts and emotions.

According to the work of Barbara Frederikson who is one of the most cited scholars in positive psychology, the ten positive emotions that offset a bad mood are love (considered the most powerful), joy, gratitude, serenity, interest, hope, pride, amusement, inspiration and awe. Since corporate America wasn't built on these positive emotions, but instead on capitalism, it is imperative that Black women and other women of color be intentional about bolstering their world and very existence with at least three of these positive emotions each day.

Know how to tap into positive emotion, even when it seems everyone doesn't like you.

So when it comes to likability, it's important to like yourself first. That requires knowing who you are and then embracing all of you, including your strengths and challenges. That implies that you must tap into the positive emotions of pride, love for yourself, and perhaps hope, which fuels goal-getting.

When Andrea Williams reaches for positive emotion, she reaches for joy, more precisely, the joy in recognizing others. As the Chief Experience Officer at the Utah Jazz, she's had to. She is one of the highest-ranking women in the male-dominated National Basketball Association and previously at the NCAA, where she was Chief Operating Officer of the College Football Playoff.

"You know, when you're not looking inward, and you're looking outward, and you're projecting positivity, and you're projecting grace and advancement for others. There's joy in that," Williams said. "And once you recognize that you can still be successful, you can still achieve things, but at the same time, recognize, celebrate, amplify, the rewards of others, there's joy in that. And it keeps your focus on something else"

Williams said that if she had known that when she was younger, it may have helped her grow and mature a little bit faster.

***

Coaching Questions

How will you apply the idea of strategic likability to move forward in your quest for senior executive leadership?

_____
_____
_____
_____
_____
_____
_____
_____
_____
_____
_____
_____
_____
_____
_____
_____
_____
_____
_____
_____
_____
_____

Which combination of positive emotions will you tap into in order to reach for happiness despite challenges in the workplace?

Finally, own the affirmation. Write it down and then add proof so that your mind can engage this positive thought with logic and reason: i.e., "I am likable and bring value to any space because... [Fill in the blank with a past experience that proves the affirmation.]

_____
_____
_____
_____
_____
_____
_____
_____
_____
_____
_____
_____
_____
_____
_____
_____
_____
_____
_____
_____
_____
_____
_____
_____

3 AFFIRMATION #2

"I WILL ATTRACT THE RIGHT SPONSORS WHO WILL OPEN DOORS FOR ME"

Secret: Some sponsors are all talk and no action. Have a plan.

I've been snowed. It's happened at least twice in my career, and it wasn't apparent to me until some time had passed. When I was in the midst of the hype, I was indeed riding high – hopeful, happy and looking forward to some really promising opportunities. It's safe to say that these sponsors were masters at gassing me up. And let's face it; when you are a double outsider who has finally caught the attention of perceived, powerful movers and shakers who have the power to take your career in the right direction, it's like striking gold. No doubt, I was putting in the work, and the fruit of my labor was not going unnoticed. I knew that the best sponsors traditionally come to you because they've seen your work firsthand or have heard the good buzz about you. When you are tapped, it is not only gratifying, but it builds you up. Women of color need external affirmation as well, although it isn't always available.

External validation from the right people that is merited is rare for double disadvantaged professionals in the workplace. Because you are othered, you are often invisible and unrecognized. These powerful people instantly become a part of your tribe because you've watched them move, you respect them and they tell you that they have your best interest in mind.

Master coach and Chief Executive Officer of the Batie Group, LaFern Kitt Batie, had this to say about sponsors who don't deliver, "It is just my philosophy, a person who's in that role of sponsor or champion for you who is not doing anything to help you move forward is really just a placeholder."

In retrospect, I liken this relationship to one with a narcissistic romantic partner. You don't have to be a psychologist to know the signs these days because the behaviors are textbook (referenceable in respected publications like *Psychology Today*) or, at least, a trending topic on TikTok. If only I had that app back then, and had the insight to apply to critical business relationships what I heard from these armchair, Tik-Tok therapists and dating coaches, I may not have fallen for their ways.

Love bombing can happen with suspect sponsors.

I will never forget how strong this one sponsor came on. Much like a new suitor who sends dozens upon dozens of roses and whisks you away on trips very early in the relationship, this senior leader was definitely saying all the right things and even dropping ideas I'd yet to even consider. The fact that s/he was especially well positioned to advocate for me and wield the influence to make it happen made it extremely difficult to see through the smoke and mirrors. I didn't realize then what I know now – that when you are excellent, you can attract the wrong leaders who are seeking their own supply. They will leverage your name for clout as social currency in their own sphere of influence. You read that right. This is why their bad behavior goes unnoticed by the most excellent and high-performing among us. We simply don't expect that someone would notice our value and then use it to their advantage. After all, it's the heft of *the sponsor's* name and reputation that the extraordinary up-and-comers are seeking in order to advance their own leadership aspirations. There is equity in our names as high-performing leaders. But it never occurred to me that there was some advantage to that leader in associating with me. This happened before I realized my own value.

However, it was clear that my star was shining brightly. I recall receiving word through the top guy's communications team to keep speaking about my work at the company and amplifying it on social media because he liked what I was doing. Similarly, this senior executive sought me out for our first meeting after hearing me speak. I was barely off the platform after holding court at an industry event when they uttered the magic words we all want to hear: "I'm going to sponsor you." I was floored. This had never happened to me before.

The wrong sponsor will use "future faking" to keep you around.

Let's be clear; getting a sponsor who is invested in you and willing to sincerely act when it counts is tough! In fact, women of color have pointed to obtaining a great mentor, let alone a single sponsor, as being one of the most challenging obstacles to their leadership aspirations. When I surveyed those 100 professional Black women, 45% of them responded that they hadn't been able to secure a reliable mentor or sponsor in their career quest. Only some 17% of them said they had a sponsor who helped them to navigate their career and make it less stressful.

While I'm not saying the two sponsors that surprised me with their ultimate lack of effectiveness or empty promises were devious by any means, reliability wouldn't be the word I'd use to describe either of them in retrospect. In both cases, I truly believe they meant well. And on the countless times we spoke by phone or in person, they indeed poured into me, affirming me, sharing words of wisdom, providing cautionary tales, showing me where the stones were and turning them when necessary. But, honestly, these are the moves of a mentor. Because a sponsor is supposed to intentionally activate, advocate and make things happen for you.

Throwing around C-suite titles, point-blank conversations about succession and talking of their conversations with the top brass to move you up the ranks really only amounts to future faking when years have passed and you've seen no results. In one case, it became apparent that one of these faux sponsors not only had access to the list of positions that were to be cut in the round of layoffs that would ultimately amount to my departure, but s/he actually had the power to do something about it. Did either of these executives harbor ill intent for me? I absolutely do not believe they did. In fact, I still call them both friends and continue to foster solid relationships with them. But over time, I was able to see that there was more talk happening than actual action.

About a year before I received that surplus notice, one of my sponsors outside of the business had not only raised my hopes about an external opportunity that would have been extremely high-profile, but we even had conversations about compensation. It would have been a sweet, sweet deal. But ultimately, when I finally received the call to discuss an actual offer, it would have been a less-than-lateral move – the same title that I currently had, and for which I was overqualified, at an organization that had only a sliver of the multibillion-dollar valuation of my current company. I would also have to report to someone with only a sliver of my experience.

I couldn't believe my ears, and I did everything in my power to hide the quivers in my voice as I spoke to the crony that was sent my way to have this insulting discussion. The role had diminished in an unbelievable way: from an officer position to a director role, reporting to someone who had been an intern less than six years before. I could tell that even the person who called me knew what she was saying was not at all appropriate based on my credentials or my experience. She was apologetic without saying so. Her tone was telling. She didn't want to be in the position to offer me what appeared to be scraps. I managed to remain composed and professional before telling her that we should remain in touch in case something changed, but when I hung up the phone, I cried like I hadn't cried in a very long time.

I felt sucker punched, and what a position to be in. The character and career assassins were out in full force at my current company, and my sponsor was fully aware. S/he tried to get me out but couldn't quite deliver in the way she said she could. I had publicly claimed this sponsor. Everyone seemed to know our relationship, and then suddenly, I'd lost so much faith in this person. I had to pray over it. My tribe knew that this opportunity would not only be my "get out of jail free" card while I was fighting a seemingly unwinnable battle at work with a chain of command that was determined to undermine my team and me, but it would have been a role that I deserved. Finally!

My close friends and family know that I claim to use my superpowers for good and not evil. And it's in times like these when you realize the power you have as an elite communicator with connections at every level of influence in the media and beyond to completely undo someone who has hurt you. However, you don't. I only shared with one confidante what really happened with that opportunity and how it ultimately went down. Even in sharing with her, I told her that I didn't believe that this sponsor meant any ill will. That said, I did believe that it was an example of someone whose mouth wrote a check that their backside ultimately couldn't cash.

In the case of both of these executives, who were absolutely friends to me through a very tough time, I look back and I'm able to clearly see what actually happened. Two things can be true at once, after all. These were well-meaning people who, for whatever reason, couldn't deliver on the things they said that they could, though they'd positioned themselves as willing and able to do. In both those cases, we probably would have all benefited if they had owned up to being purely mentors or even simply great confidants. Because, when all is said and done, a sponsor is supposed to deliver results and not gigantic helpings of nothing or disappointment.

Ultimately, however, I was blessed to have just the opposite of these unreliable sponsors: true sponsors flying under the radar as mentors. It was completely unexpected because these senior leaders positioned themselves as mentors, real advisors, but occasionally cashed in figurative checks that not only cleared but had a few extra zeros added to the total remittance. Those quiet actions truly made a difference in my leadership goals, but so did my savviness to have a plan all my own.

"If you have someone who's in that role and they're not supporting you, but it's politically beneficial to have that person remain in that space, understand it," Batie said. "Keep it for the visual and then leverage those who are really going to open doors for you, asking questions of them, getting insights about their experiences, asking them about areas that you are unfamiliar with."

Since unreliable sponsors aren't always obvious at the start, it's best to have a plan all your own to preserve your happiness.

I'd been let down by a sponsor before. However, the first time that happened, I was dependent on the outcome of their actions with no other recourse. You see, I'm an optimist, and when I was younger, I trusted everything my respected senior leaders said that I should. They had the character, the clout and the power to make things happen, so why not?

I'm reminded of the quote from Dr. Martin Luther King, Jr. that is emblazoned in the hearts and minds of any 90s hip-hop enthusiast because we loved Public Enemy and a certain Spike Lee Joint.

"Yet our best trained, best educated, best prepared troops refuse to fight. Matter of fact, it's safe to say they'd rather switch...than fight."---Martin Luther King, Jr.

When you have settled in with the idea that not all sponsors can and will affect change for you, you must engage in self-advocacy, thinking ahead to a course that you've set for yourself despite what a sponsor may or may not be able to achieve for you. I could have been completely devastated had I only fixed my sights on that dream role that the one sponsor said s/he had for me. However, I had been interviewing at other places and had started a business outside of my current role at the company. I did not "place all of my eggs in one basket," as my grandmother would have called it.

Understanding that some sponsors cannot or will not deliver for you is a fact that few people discuss, focusing only on the idea that you should obtain a sponsor. The implication is that they will always act on your behalf and be effective. The truth is, sometimes, that simply isn't the case.

Sponsorship impotency is real.

I've been exploring in conversations with my Black women leader clients how the watering, dimming and culturally dumbing down of Black leaders on their way up the corporate ladder can cause what I call "sponsorship impotency." I wanted to know how it impacts the Black women and other women of color that they say they sponsor. It is very painfully described in stark dialogue in a clip of the 1972 movie Trick Baby that TikTok creators recently resurrected to spur a conversation on "the plan" to groom Black professionals so that they yearn to be more like their white counterparts – so that they lack the desire to fight back against a system that they know was built to exclude them. The scene seems harmless enough at first glance – people dressed in their finery, dining on the finest. But then, the intentionally cunning cinematography begins to reveal the true context. The service staff is all Black and smiling brightly. The dinner guests are all white, with only white men driving the conversation. The focal point is two men, who represent liberal and conservative views, critiquing each other on how effective or ineffective their approaches are to keeping Black people unmotivated to fight and even become their allies. I watched TikTok creators reacting to the videos, eyes widening with every matter-of-fact statement shared in the light-hearted banter, seeing how the discussion never impacted the Cheshire Cat smiles on the faces of the Black maids and butlers. That clip spilled over onto Linkedin, where I saw it first. The commentary on that business social media platform was even more detailed and deconstructing in nature because of how the written word is centered over rich content on the platform. You get an overwhelming 2200+ character count on Linkedin, while video-centric platforms like TikTok and IG Reels only provide you with a few minutes of video time to get the point across.

The commentary that I saw ran the gamut, from sentiments like "Who is really running the show here?" to "Black people need to wake up" to even "They promoted you because you have been neutralized."

These neutralized Black leaders, and even the Asian and LatinX ones, can completely leave a BIPOC leader blowing in the wind with promises of pipe dreams, promotions and succession. This may be one of the many reasons why so many Black women professionals who want to lead in a significant way can't identify a sponsor for themselves. Those leaders of color who can say that they have a sponsor whisper to one another about how some sponsors of color lack the impact they desire on their leadership aspirations because they are "agreeable."

Of course, you can point to the sheer lack of women of color at the top of the Fortune 500, let alone Black women in the C-Suite, to determine why there are so few powerful and effective sponsors out there that look like those aspiring Black women leaders. But add in why the handful that do exist may be so ineffective, and it may be yet another reason why most women point to white male sponsors as having the most impact on their careers.

In an episode of the hit show Black-ish, Rainbow (Bow) Johnson, a high-ranking doctor, seeks comradery with more junior doctors in two very awkward and unfortunate scenarios: once over a break during the day and another at a happy hour that she orchestrated. During the latter, it became painfully obvious how removed and unfamiliar she was with the younger Black women doctors' experiences, and she was also, in fact, unsympathetic and unwilling to empathize with their plight. She was so embedded in the corporate culture of that health system that she could no longer recognize herself in the young Black women doctors. Indeed, she eventually adopted a chastising tone suggesting that they had to earn their stripes.

The chasm that this episode insightfully demonstrated between Black women in the executive ranks and those in the rank and file underscored the reality of the canyon that forms between high-ranking professional Black women and the more junior ones. The senior executive laments that her peers, who are mostly white males, do not accept her and her inability to relate to the more junior Black women who are trying to ultimately become her. Bow, who is half white, struggles throughout the series to always fully see the struggle of Black people because her life experience afforded her some privilege (and some pain) to which Black people, who weren't of mixed heritage, couldn't relate.

Vanilla Black people can trip you on your way up the ladder.

I was on the line with a client recently who was sharing concerns about some organizational changes that would impact her role. It seemed her boss hadn't given any thought to it. Her boss had moved up. She was left to fend for herself and pick up the pieces in the department where her boss had originally hired her. That part of the business wasn't exactly well-run. In fact, it was a bit of a mess. She described her boss as nice and pretty. In her view, her boss's work was less than extraordinary. It was simply okay, but the word that she used that struck me was "agreeable." Easy on the eyes, with a relationship with the man at the top who had a reputation as a hatchet man and who was no real friend to Black employees, my client called her manager…*agreeable*. Listening to her reflect on her current situation, the thought occurred to me:

The power center rewards the most vanilla Black folk. They are boring and lackluster. If they are incredibly smart, they hide it well. They try their best to blend in and assimilate, and they are certainly *vanilla!* But be aware that one can be chocolate and still be vanilla through and through. After all, who doesn't like vanilla? It's safe, mild and draws within the lines. It's dependable. Vanilla Bean, Homemade Vanilla or French Vanilla are vaguely nuanced flavors, yet very much the same. You may not love it, but you don't hate it either.

This safe flavor that they bring to every situation is typically on full display around their white bosses, though sometimes it's disguised with the people who could really use their support, advocacy and sponsorship. It's not how they disguise it; it's why they disguise it that's at issue. But let's explore why it is important that they don't show their vanilla status to other people of color whom they outrank.

Referring back to that episode with Dr. Rainbow Johnson, she unleashed every Black idiom and African-American Vernacular English (AAVE) she could muster, making those Black women doctors visibly uncomfortable. In my experience, senior executives like Dr. Bow want other Black professionals to believe that they are actually there to help them based on their position. But in some cases, they have to reach to position themselves as relatable when they choose not to be aloof.

You see, some of us believe that if we are agreeable in the white gaze, we are safe. But this is a different kind of safe. It isn't the kind of safe that benefits the vanilla Black folks or the people around them who look to them for sponsorship or mentorship. It is the kind of safe that benefits the power center. In fact, this kind of safe is really a weaponization of people of color in power who present as sounding boards, resources and advocates. They can do more to undo you by saying and acting as if they've got your back, when in truth, their inaction and impotency can destroy your aspirations.

Vanilla Black folk in high places battle their own fears. Now that they are seemingly in the circle, they must protect that position at all costs. The interest of the people they claim to mentor or sponsor will never come before their own. If it aligns with their interests, well, today, you're in luck, but perhaps not tomorrow. As much as they probably would never admit it in public, only to their spouses before saying goodnight (as Dr. Bow did with her husband Dre in the sitcom), they are othered even on the corporate jets, in the boardrooms and the creamy center. Those spaces are simply a microcosm of the larger corporate ecosystem, only in close quarters.

Sitting with a client, who works at a giant pharmaceutical company, one weekday morning over coffee, she shared with me some ideas about potential sponsors who might be able to help her with her leadership aspirations. As we strategized, she was able to uncover at least two Black women senior leaders who were already advocates. As she continued to share how extraordinary they were, she began to talk about how these advocates, people who "should have been promoted long ago," still had struggles. These Black women were making it to the final round, down to two people sometimes, only to miss out on promotion, with no real explanation. These were women who had metaphorically parted the Red Seas of the corporate world, turned the water of the corporate wells into wine and accomplished amazing things by founding new businesses and business resource groups, innovating and problem-solving. However, they were still trying to move up from middle management. They were superheroes, the She-Hulks and Captain Marvels of the workplace. They were the kind of women whose miraculous work and heavy lifts preceded them. Everyone knew their highly publicized accomplishments and accolades. People could call these women by name and sing their praises, yet, they were still stuck. Recounting their stories was exciting at first, but the realization set in that even these mavens, these Dora Milaje of corporate America with their agility and exceptional skills, were indeed in limbo. And, if these women were working miracles by their own hands and hadn't been moved up, what's the outlook for others who merely and simply outshine their colleagues?

So I had to dig into this a little deeper. These women, the only ones in their divisions at one of the largest pharmas in the world, indeed had the sponsorship, but I would soon learn they had sponsors who looked like them. However, isn't that the dream? Isn't that what we are told to look for? Seek out sponsors who are Black, accomplished, respected and willing to support. It's the absolute Holy Grail because these Black unicorns just simply don't exist according to the numbers. Only 41 women lead Fortune 500 companies, and only 7% of those are women of color, among which only two of them are Black. So to find one, even one who simply has a C-level title, is an accomplishment in and of itself. Even locating a Black man is a once-in-a-lifetime sighting. I mean, we only get to see one or two of the Seven Wonders of the World in our lifetime. This is the eighth! And to find someone willing to offer support, who does not solely seem to be out for their own interests? Well, that, my sister, is a miracle from the Lord Himself.

So these Black women she described had not only identified these Black sponsors, they'd lassoed them. And yet, there was not a promotion in sight after several attempts.

It begged the question, as the youngsters would say: "How, Sway?" How could this be? We tossed around all sorts of ideas. Perhaps the business needs to be shifted? Perhaps someone was already tagged for the role – you know, the insider that simply got the jump because they were pre-identified? Maybe there was some act of God? The answer to all these questions was clearly no. Then why, exactly? How could these waymakers, miracle workers, promise keepers, lights in the darkness get down to the final two candidates out of hundreds, with premium Black sponsorship but ultimately get passed over? The answer lies in the identity of the sponsors, who self-selected to bang their fists on a table and see around corners these for Black women but couldn't raise their names in rooms where they weren't.

You see, although these Black sponsors have ascended into the creamy center, they too are othered, simply in closer quarters. Their word doesn't mean as much. Their effort doesn't carry the same weight. Their fist banging on a table? Well, that, to some, is still angry. These Black sponsors are still not centered, and the fact is that they haven't arrived, and they never will. They may have more money, a better title and great perks, but mostly it's hush money.

How much are they really willing to risk to help move another brother or sister up? These are the risks they must mitigate. However, once in a very blue moon, you might find one without much to lose, but they are typically close to retirement or otherwise have one foot out the door.

So could it be that some of these impotent sponsors of color could very well be blowing smoke? There are those who absolutely put in the effort until they hit a brick wall, but others engage in a game that has more to do with maintaining the *image* of helping other professionals of color climb the corporate ladder. I submit, however, if it is indeed smoke and mirrors, time is your best indication of who they truly are. Because even when a house is set ablaze, once the fire dies down, soon the smoke will too.

Time is the best way to assess the real ones.

It took me years to figure out that you certainly have to watch the actions of others and compare them to the image they've formed in your head. When you realize that everyone is human, everyone is flawed, and everyone eventually has to do the same thing you do after digesting their food, then you can begin to deconstruct your rose-colored fantasies about the people you admire. After all, something about these people must be special to make it this far. Is it magic? Were they selected because they were the most agreeable? Yes, they probably did have to be ten times better to get where they are, but now that they are there, are they still? And their stature says nothing of their character. In fact, in many cases, their political acumen may be so sharp and intense that you may be surprised at how cutthroat they might actually be beneath the facade, no doubt primarily to survive and maintain their position, but also on behalf of their company.

The reality is that at some point, the higher you ascend, the more sold out you become for that company's interests, secondarily to your own. For someone with character, this will come with a clear expiration date. For others, it's an indication to draw the check until they push you out. As for those who fail but at least seem to mean well when they say they are going to work to get you that role, opportunity or stretch assignment, it's important to protect yourself from them moving forward and not allow them to practice on your career ever again. You see, I would hold out hope based on my respect and admiration for these sponsors, but on a couple of occasions in my career, it put me in a real pinch. I had no backup plan because I trusted them. But believe me, the lesson was in the chaos it created, and in the buckling down to rebuild and eventually do what I needed for myself, because I could.

Perhaps this is where we fail ourselves, believing that these sponsors have all the power. We're defeated before we begin. Speaking with a fellow professor and consultant and former Chief Learning Officer for the Executive Leadership Council, it was revealed to me that sponsorship is the most elusive and crucial element to the rise into the C-Suite. Dr. Christopher C. Butts told me that most Black women just don't know what they don't know and are surprised at how tough the ascension is. He said that these women really aren't prepared for what they face once they get there.

"There's great awareness around the potential challenges and hardships that might take place to obtain those C-suite positions. However, I think what we hear is that it was so much more difficult or so much more challenging than even what they anticipated and expected, knowing that they've had conversations, read research and done all sorts of preparation for those positions," Butts said. "But I think it's been quite interesting to hear that it's even more challenging than they anticipated to ascend to those levels. And the reason for that is there's just sort of that, that black ceiling effect where the information, gosh, the information just isn't shared with them. And the sponsorship is not present. The amount of development opportunities do not present themselves for black women. And with that, it's sort of, you know, I don't know what I don't know."

Is it that we, as Black women, are looking for sponsorship love in all the wrong places? That we are on the hunt for the Black unicorn sponsor to wave their magic wands and make something happen for us? Perhaps, the unlikely lake that we should be fishing in, though it seems counterintuitive, is ripe with people who don't look like us, who will step up and make things happen.

What happens when we inadvertently fumble a sponsor relationship

Sometimes, my Sister, it isn't the sponsor. It's us. And I'm not talking about the tropes that say we need more executive presence or that perhaps we need to be a bit more "buttoned up." I'm talking about when we are in that room or at that table and we don't know how to "talk the talk" to sustain and make the most out of the new relationship.

Dr. Diana B. Allen, an empowerment champion and senior cyber security expert, who researched women in technology and sponsorship with a particular eye on Black women, told me that in her research of women in tech, she saw that Black women and even their white counterparts displayed the same pattern. They would secure the sponsor, but a year later, they were moved out of the organization, or they left on their own. She said that it isn't that we don't have the same access as men, we simply don't always know what to do next, and there are simply certain things we must know when we get there.

"I think calibration, consensus, situational awareness," Allen said. "And so what tends to happen to women? So, now I'm in this role, I'm here, I'm in the room, and folks are like, all right. You made it to the room. Good seeing you. Good job. Now you're one of us. That's a lie. It's not true."

She said that women leaders need to know what to ask for when we speak to sponsors. They need to understand the language of the business and how they can impact it. Women leaders need to understand what a mandate is and how to obtain it, what calibration is, and how those rooms work. They need to be able to strike up conversations about succession or at least be well-positioned so that the sponsor initiates that dialogue. The precursor to these conversations, Dr. Allen said, is excellence and performance excellence that your sponsors and their peers are aligned on.

Questions about one's competency need to be a thing of the past. Dr. Allen laments that too often, Black women, seduced by internet culture and social media, believe that the concept of "black girl magic" has misled many into thinking that they are entitled to these conversations and sponsorship simply because they exist, avoiding the hard work, hard questions and tough-love conversations that mentors can share if they are listened to. Eagles listen, apply the learning and soar because they are willing to do the work.

Allen added, "I agree with the chickens and the eagles, but when you get there, it's gonna take, you know, everything you've got."

Coaching Questions

How will you shift your mindset and actions at the prospect of new sponsorship so that your career outcome doesn't depend solely on your sponsor's actions or lack of action?

_____
_____
_____
_____
_____
_____
_____
_____
_____
_____
_____
_____
_____
_____
_____
_____
_____
_____
_____
_____
_____
_____

How will you open yourself up to more sponsorship that may not look like you moving forward?

_____
_____
_____
_____
_____
_____
_____
_____
_____
_____
_____
_____
_____
_____
_____
_____
_____
_____
_____
_____
_____
_____
_____
_____
_____

L. Michelle Smith

When you have made it to executive senior leadership or the C-Suite, how will you approach sponsorship differently after reading this chapter?

_____
_____
_____
_____
_____
_____
_____
_____
_____
_____
_____
_____
_____
_____
_____
_____
_____
_____
_____
_____
_____
_____
_____
_____
_____

***

4 AFFIRMATION #3

"I AM WORTHY OF EXECUTIVE COMPENSATION SO THAT I CAN BUILD GENERATIONAL WEALTH"

Secret: Certain wealth-building opportunities only present themselves to professionals after they achieve a certain level in corporate America. The key is to reach that level, and it isn't as high as you might think.

According to a University of Pennsylvania Wharton Business School study, the popular saying, "Money can't buy you happiness," isn't necessarily true. The 2021 research revealed that happiness does, in fact, increase the more money people make. The bottom line: money affords people the ability to make choices about how they live their lives. Could it be that conventional wisdom has set some of us back?

How you made more money was different in agency life than in the towers of the Fortune 500. You worked your way up to partner in most firms, and then it was all about profit sharing. Until then, you focused on the raise, the promotion and the bonus – end of story. Client-side was a whole different animal. No one really says it out loud, but ultimately, there is a level that holds the golden key to executive compensation. What I found intriguing was that it wasn't simply Black women; I even saw older white men and everyone in between find their way into management and simply stay there until retirement. It was as if they found a comfortable spot on the corporate ladder that was, at the very least, consistent; the path of less resistance. As my grandmother would say about others like them, "They wouldn't kill anything or let anything die." They would simply collect their check every pay cycle, accept the incremental raise each year and the lump sum bonus if someone thought they earned it. Then every year, the exact same process happened until it was time to retire.

Let's face it: This is the life that so many in the corporate realm have accepted, and ultimately, it is what keeps the engines of big business turning at a very steady and predictable clip. After all, not everyone can be in the C-Suite, right? It also means that, for one reason or another, we don't all have the same aspirations. It is, however, safe to say that this behavior, generation over generation, produces lineages of workhorses and foot soldiers, the dependable workers. But it also means we aren't producing generation over generation of American executive leadership primed for the C-Suite. It can be argued that someone, somewhere, intentionally structured it this way – that if the average white person isn't making it to the top of the Fortune 500, people of color are probably conditioned even more so to stay within the ranks and be content.

I honestly can't say that I always knew that I wanted to run something. I do believe that watching my mother teach for most of my childhood and young adulthood and then watching my father give his entire career to the Federal Government as a civil servant did reveal some pronounced messages to me. One of them was that if you worked hard, you could do more than get by. You could save in the long term and achieve the American Dream, which by any measure, is actually fairly basic.

But can we be real for a minute? The idea that the American Dream is a dream for those of us with advanced degrees and healthy six-figure incomes is a misconception. Sure, if you immigrated with nothing and worked your way up with blue-collar jobs and a mom-and-pop business, then owning a home is definitely a dream worth celebrating once you attain it. If you were in my parent's generation, those who lived through part of Jim Crow and the Civil Rights Movement, of course their dream is worth having, and when you achieve it, you could be proud. But how is it that educated people with healthy salaries and white and platinum-collar careers still buy into this paradigm as their dream too? It is the basics, table stakes, the baseline. As a person of color, you may face some discrimination along the way, but you could tolerate it and still pull a healthy six figures to ultimately improve your lifestyle.

As always, it's cultural.

My father has always liked nice cars. And while I cannot say that we always had a nice one, we always bought a new one when he'd finished paying off the older one. When we were really living "the dream," he would trade up. Eventually, he bought a Cadillac Coupe de Ville – arguably the Black church folks' dream car. Even GM knew that. Ford too. Black people had a wonderful relationship with cars because they opened the doors to cross-country travel with dignity. If you traveled at the right times and took the right highways, you could avoid being harassed or demeaned as you could be on mass transit like trains and buses. My family's progress in life could be tracked with the upgrades in our driveway. My sister and I both graduated from private school. Mind you, absolutely not the most expensive one, but it was a Christian academy – not exactly Roosevelt High School, the public high school about a mile away where one of my uncles coached basketball for a while. That high school was located in the projects. My sister and I wore uniforms to our private school.

And then, we attended *that* church, one of those that, back in the 50s, one of the most influential members of the Southern Baptist Convention called out in a speech to that body that demonstrated the reason why keeping Sunday morning services and, therefore, all churches in the South segregated wasn't hurting anyone. He pointed to row after row of fine cars in the parking lots and the many elaborate and intricate church hats, fine suits and furs that paraded inside each Sunday. It was Dallas's original megachurch, Good Street Baptist Church, and its sister church, St. John Missionary Baptist Church, was only a few miles away. Yes, we attended Good Street.

I remember the first time we went. Mama took us both by the hand and we walked. That was less about us not having a car, but more about her experience in Arkansas, walking to church on dirt roads in her one Sunday dress. In her mind, this was a "come up." We had several dresses and Mary Janes, Lazy Bones albeit, paved roads and some grassy knolls. So, praise the Lord and keep it steppin'!

I didn't like arriving at church in a sweat. Eventually, Daddy drove us in the station wagon. A few years later, he drove us in the brand-new Oldsmobile 98. When that one was paid off, he traded it for the Cadillac. Our transportation to church got better and better. By the time I enrolled at Texas Christian University, which my parents had made abundantly clear was unaffordable, Daddy was promoted in his civil servant position. By the time I was a sophomore at the university, they could better afford tuition at the private, predominately white institution (PWI).

So, parents who never showed even a streak of true ambition the way we know it today (in fact, that was seen as a somewhat sinful concept), but instead displayed unprecedented resilience, grit and stick-to-it-ness, were able to make good, hard-working, modest strides through perseverance. They placed a heavy emphasis on savings and home ownership but not on investing, besides buying bonds and CDs. They also leveled a steady rebuke on name brands (except for cars). So it follows that I came up believing that work was simply a means to an end, not a journey to a dream beyond the basics.

This probably explains why I have never skimped when I purchased a car. And I found it odd when people lingered too long on the topic with me or raised an eyebrow about what I might be driving. We owned our cars, never leased. We paid them off. We took care of them like most people take care of their pets. It's just who we are. But we never saw them as status symbols, and neither my sister nor I had ambitions to run a huge company. It just wasn't in our experience. We couldn't "be it" because we didn't "see it." But we both bought Saabs when we did make our first car purchase on our own. And while our friends were buying and leasing Hondas, we were also purchasing our first homes. As single women in our mid-20s, we were different. Both of us matriculated from PWIs, and those fine church people let us know that we were outsiders. To be on the inside, perhaps we should have driven Japanese economy cars and enrolled at a Historically Black College or University (HBCU). For the record, both of my parents went to one. Let it be known that I still regret not being able to attend myself.

But then I saw something that challenged it all. I saw women running the offices at the global agencies where I cut my teeth in strategic communication. It would be the first time I'd see women with nannies taking charge and sitting at tables with men, calling the shots. That was the first time I asked myself if that was what I wanted. It wasn't like what I witnessed at home, so it was foreign. But they promoted me, and I recall that I intentionally sought a promotion twice in my career. That was so different from what my parents ever did. I remember asking my SVP what it would take to make VP at the firm, and she was very open about it. So much so that I did what she said, and about a year later, she promoted me to VP. I wasn't even 30 years old. There was a nice pay increase and some bonuses that I had access to that I hadn't in the past. That's when I had the 5-series shipped from Germany. It would dock a month later, and I was excited to drive "Silver" for the next 11 years.

I was doing well. I bought my first home as a Senior Account Executive before that. I bought my Saab, "The Green Hornet," when I signed on with the TV station before that. My progress was steady, and I was slowly building a little wealth, although I wasn't taught to see it that way. It was framed as "security." But nothing prepared me for what compensation would be like in a $140 billion organization with 280,000+ employees. They could pay me exactly what I was making as an SVP at another global firm, but they couldn't (translate wouldn't) give me the title to go with it. I entered as a senior manager. At the time, it was fine. I surmised I had twenty years in the industry already. It wasn't a job that I was looking for exactly. It literally fell into my lap, and although I did press for a director title several times, I was told that the role wasn't "scoped" for that. I didn't know what that meant other than they hadn't budgeted for director pay. That was enough to let me know that I needed to get to that level as soon as possible.

Let's pause in the story for a minute. I've often reflected on that moment and I wondered how far back I put myself in earning potential and title when I accepted the senior manager role. It wouldn't be the first time a woman had placed a salary over a title when accepting a role. Career experts say without fail that a job title not only impacts your current work but also influences your future work and career trajectory. Back then, had I considered the crucial implications of job titles and known my value (which wasn't a part of the "work hard and live a modest life" paradigm that I was accustomed to), I would have understood that, especially as I wasn't pressed for a new job, I could have held out for a better title and pay elsewhere.

"It eternally impacts your wealth." The Batie Group founder LaFern Kit Batie said. "If I go in and I've negotiated a lower salary, fewer stock options, no retention bonus, without all the perks that don't take money out of my pocket, but take them out of the company's pocket, then it eternally impacts my wealth."

Her advice is to slow down, and if the opportunity is going to disappear in 24 to 48 hours, then you have to ask yourself how solid an opportunity it is. I should have slowed down, and this is something I encourage my clients to do when the stakes are much higher. I recall one client shared that she accepted a C-Suite role before negotiating the salary and later found out that she could have received 50% more than she did.

Dr. Diana B. Allen also noticed the pattern of women placing a premium on compensation over title.

"We tend to get into roles and say, I don't care what they call me, as long as they pay me on time, as long as they pay me the type of money that I want to make," Allen said. "I'm not focused on titles because we're encouraged to be humble and, you know, all of these things."

But she said that approach to negotiation is Black women's undoing when it comes to sustainable influence in rooms that matter. She shared that women tend to get "squishy" titles that aren't as well-defined or as powerful as men. Titles like "Lead" this and "Global Head" of that really don't fall into the traditional structure. In her search for women who qualified for her study, she found women with these ambiguous titles that didn't speak to their power and influence and men who had definitive titles like VP of this or Chief that.

"So what tends to happen in those roles when you have the 'I don't care what they call me, as long as they pay me appropriately' [mindset] is you miss certain elements that are granted with positional authority," Allen said. "And so that comes with access to certain rooms, participation in conversation, access to information. And so those are components of empowerment. Certain rooms are restricted based on level, and so they make up this level in between where you should be and where you are. But you know, you're not a senior manager. Or you're not a director, but you're not a senior director. You're now a global lead of something in between that, which is something new that we've created just for you. Where does that put you in the overall hierarchy and pipeline?"

Mismatched titles can make for more than money trouble.

Before I was promoted to that director role, the trouble started. Youngsters with my same job title looked at me curiously. They thought I moved differently. I traded "Silver" for "Smokey," a brand new X5, only months after taking the position. My looks didn't tell the full story, either. I looked 30ish, maybe younger, and I had a newborn. I was in my early 40s, although no one could tell, and in the words of my immediate boss at the time, "You move like a VP."

I couldn't help it. I *was* a VP…when I was 29, a CEO in my 30s, and SVP when I was 40. I walked differently, alright, and they didn't like it. The VPs there liked it, however. They were all ten years my senior, but there was something about me. We spoke the same language. I was walking among eagles, but planted among chickens, thanks to a mismatched title. This would come to a head before I left the organization, but before it did, I managed to do something that I was told was next to impossible. I was promoted within the same role for which I was hired.

You see, there was something that my boss, the original hiring manager, told me about how the role wasn't scoped for a director.

What he wasn't saying was that a director receives executive compensation. That meant that I would instantly have access to stocks, merit bonuses and lump sums over and above what I'd see as a senior manager, as well as other benefits that were otherwise invisible to anyone in a lower band. There was even a separate executive compensation portal with access to stock trading and managing my pension and other pockets of privilege (translation: money). Not only had I been told that moving up in that company usually meant moving into another role, but I was also told that making the leap from senior manager to director was the most difficult jump to make.

In my case, a whole new director role had to be created above me and funded. They eliminated the senior manager role I once filled and used that budget to get my first full-time team members – a couple of lead consultants. My manager had to argue that while I managed agency team members, the full-time equivalents (FTE) added up to the requirement of managing at least two reports. I was managing at least five FTEs at that point.

I was learning secrets I hadn't even sought out, and the boss who facilitated my promotion was one of the most transparent I could ever have. He explained to me why the associate director just wouldn't do it as a title. It was a vanity title that carried no pay increase and no real expansion of responsibility. It was in the same band as a senior manager. He explained that I wanted to get that director title because it put me into this brand-new executive compensation realm.

What did executive compensation *really* mean to me?

Besides the fact that directors had more clout and respect with the VPs and officers in the company (meaning I could sit at tables with them, and they would take my counsel without calling my boss about it), being a director meant that I had crossed over into the corporate promised land of executive compensation. In this world, you could pile up stock that would vest over time, and if the company was doing well in the market, this meant an incredible nest egg was just sitting there, accruing value. Access to that stock only required great performance, and the company had to perform well for you to get other classes of stock, profit sharing and lump sum bonuses paid out over time. So, if you consider someone who stayed with the company for more than 15 years, even if they never made VP, chances are that the stocks and other perks that they accrued could literally set them up for life. That is before you count their 401K pension (which is nearly extinct these days) and even life and other insurance packages that were nothing to sneeze at.

Despite the tax implications, all of the above represents wealth. The kind of wealth that sets up kids for college and elders for retirement. It's the kind of wealth that can be strategically used for other investments, like real estate, lucrative investments and other business ventures.

Mine would be the latter leading to the others. Even after leaving the big company and being surplused nearly four years ago, I still receive payouts from this company. Even though I was only there six years and only at the executive compensation level for about half that time, that's still pretty amazing. My coaching consultancy and media company is literally the company that the big company built with the stock and bonus payouts that haven't yet dried up. So my decision to leave wasn't only because I had opportunities from other companies and had this seedling of a business that I'd started; it was also a calculated financial one.

The startup investments this business needed would come directly from the executive compensation payouts I received while getting "exceeds ratings" multiple times, and I would take the proof of my good work at that company directly to the bank. In fact, my daughter's children's book *No Thanks for Girls: 7 Ways to Say I'm Beautiful, Strong and Enough* was produced by an imprint built with some of those funds, and that book will continue to accrue royalties for many years to come–*for her*.

It is safe to say that this money not only bought happiness, it *secured* my happiness past my employment and helped me weather a layoff that could have been detrimental if I didn't have a plan and some reserves. This was only made possible through my performance at my previous company. I built my home from the ground up as I was promoted to director at that company. And thanks to my hard work there and recognition, I still live in that house.

I take pride that "Big Black," my latest ride, was purchased with Black dollars, hence the name, from a clientele who felt that my message and mission resonated with them – leaders who needed the support of someone who looked like them and had the same experience as them. But I definitely couldn't have purchased her if those investments hadn't laid the groundwork for my business. Reaching my original compensation level from the company and exceeding that within nine months of leaving probably wouldn't have been possible without it, either. The truth is that you must have money to make money. And if that Wharton research holds true, that can translate into the idea that you must have happiness (security to live the life you want to live) to secure more happiness.

The previous generation's model of "the good work ethic" just doesn't work in today's context.

That corporate worker who is simply happy to retire from management after 15-25 years of working at the same level at the same company is dead. It will not necessarily help you to secure your next level of happiness. Not only because it makes sense to at least move into a band level that will afford you the executive compensation that will help you discover opportunities to build generational wealth, but because companies are simply not planning to keep workers for more than 3-5 years moving into the future.

It is time for the most credentialed and highly educated group, Black women, according to the 2020 Census, to be savvy about their time in corporate. Yes, start the business on the side. Yes, leap even when you are pushed. But it is important that you ensure that you optimize your time in those corporate towers. That means getting as much knowledge, increased earning potential and monetary value from your time there before you exit.

Batie says she often receives unapologetic phone calls from men asking for her advice on how to negotiate the best offers for themselves, but not as many calls come to her from women.

"I know that if you don't get it coming in, it is hard to catch up," she said. "It is impossible to catch up."

So, what does she say to a woman who says she doesn't care about the title as long as she gets the compensation? She challenges them with a classic coaching technique. She asks them to consider what their future selves will think about an outcome if one of her peers with the title and the compensation betters her. It allows them to visualize the consequences and imagine what that could feel like.

So many of us are considering the moment and not the long-term impact. They say hindsight is 20/20. I submit that it's in 4K, high definition. While I don't spend too much time looking back, I'm now able to see professionals who started working ten years later than I did in the C-Suite. I can only assume that they also acquired the compensation they deserve, but the reality is that I'm not alone.

I was definitely "in the moment" when I accepted the position at the big company at a level far below my pay grade. My earning potential held steady, but I put myself back tremendously when I settled for the role. Do I have regrets? Well, that would likely be the only one because the opportunities my VP-level performance afforded me were priceless. The exposure I obtained, the company I kept, the corporate jet that I flew on and the leadership development I received, I wouldn't trade that for the world.

Ultimately, it brought me to where I am today, and that is absolutely amazing.

The correct answer is "both-and," not "either-or."

Why do we, especially women, believe that "both-and" is asking too much? Why do we settle for either a title or compensation far too often? Why are we okay with that? "Because we'd have to ask for it. We'd have to have an uncomfortable conversation that says, 'Here's the value I bring to the organization. I want to be competent relative to my value,'" Batie said. "If you are the CEO of your opportunities, it is your responsibility to bring your portfolio to the table. But a part of it is that pride of not having to ask for something. Again, we'll go back to it. It's the fear."

In addition to pride, fear of an uncomfortable conversation, and not knowing or being able to articulate our value, I also have some ideas about why women, especially those of us who happen to be of color, do not negotiate or ask for what we are worth in terms of title and compensation.

We are worn down. Tired!

Negotiating can seem like one more battle that we just aren't willing to fight when we have to do battle on a daily basis simply to be seen, heard, considered and not discounted simply for entering a room and existing.

We tend to make decisions based on feelings and not necessarily data and facts.

Before you say this is a stereotype about women, I admit that I have done this. Men do it, too, if they are honest with themselves. How often have we had so much going on in our lives, pressures, and even ongoing issues with our spouses and family that sometimes we simply go with what we are feeling in the moment? Sometimes, it's subconscious. I know for certain that when I'm happy, feeling positive and things are going well in life, I make better decisions. I take the time to look into all the variables, possible results and outcomes patiently and thoroughly and move more intentionally.

Society has groomed us to discount our desires, especially in business, because it wasn't built with us in mind.

Essentially, many of us have decided that we weren't built for it either. I remember working at a global agency where my EVP would invite other officers and me to her country club to grab a bite at lunch and discuss client business. Once, over a wedge salad, she told me that she liked the country club but disliked the culture simultaneously. This was a white woman, mind you.

She didn't like the angst she had each time "the tennis skirts" walked by and, ever so passive-aggressively, never outright, engaged in low-key teasing her about being a working woman. These were the ladies who lunched, women who basked in the fact that they were spending their husbands' money. They were well taken care of. The most they worried about was what to wear that day and whether they'd miss their nail appointments if they lunched for too long with the ladies.

Women pressure each other about these things. I see moms side-eyeing other moms about their choices to stay at home with the kids or have a career that may preempt the baking of cupcakes or buying them from a store. We need to be honest. It isn't always the men who are pressuring us to think of ourselves in one way and one way only. We do it ourselves. And that tiny committee of gremlins and boogie men in our heads retain a front-row seat in our minds when we question if we have our priorities right.

Imagine, if white women feel this way, how women of color could possibly feel? Whether you are Black, Hispanic or Asian, the idea of staying close to home, being the glue to your nuclear and extended family and nurturing everything is a value that goes deep into the generations. We compare ourselves to our mothers and grandmothers, who didn't have careers. We sometimes buy into the idea that if we aren't cooking all the meals, cleaning the entire house, caring for our husbands, hand and foot and being the always-on mother to our children, we are somehow betraying our womanhood.

Lately, the idea of business boss babes, i.e., lady bosses, has come into vogue. Yet some patriarchal images of womanhood persist. As I scroll through social media, I see women admonishing other women that if they are seeking a partner, those partners should be those who will not only support but fund a solopreneurial model in businesses that will be home-based, while still expecting the same level of housekeeping, child-bearing, cooking and catering they may have witnessed from their mothers and grandmothers. This despite the fact that these women were born into a time when business opportunities didn't exactly abound for them, and they felt beholden to their husbands, who were the sole breadwinners.

I married a man who had a real issue with me wanting a housekeeper. Even though, whether running a business or not, I'd had one for years before marrying him. Because my job kept me on the road and up late hunched over a laptop, it did my spirit and peace of mind good to walk into a clean, organized, and disinfected house. Does anyone else love the smell of Pine Sol? It meant I didn't constantly have to worry about picking up a broom, making a bed or clearing dishes while preparing for a multi-million dollar new business pitch, or being on call for clients who tended to beep or buzz me late at night.

His point of view was likely due in part to what his mother modeled. At the time, she was an unmarried school teacher who didn't work during the summer months and catered to his every whim. She "had never" had a housekeeper. For him, that was the end of the story.

At the time, I was expecting my daughter. I was sick each morning, commuting ninety minutes or more to my agency job (one of those demanding positions in a toxic environment) and lunching at country clubs with my boss. Oh, and by the way, earning nearly double what he was. Still, he had zero reservations about telling me he couldn't stand it. So how did we eventually align on the topic of a housekeeper? I had to pay for the housekeeper with my money. He would have nothing to do with it.

Our partners and family members will many times dissuade us from wanting more because we're "the glue" in the household or it's threatening the status quo.

Let's be clear, someone benefits from us not being aspirational in our careers, and mind you, it's typically the one who hollers the loudest when we begin to dream or walk in it. In the case of my ex, it was more about the image he concocted in his head about what a woman's role actually was in his world – a cook and a cleaning lady. If not, he at least wanted to see me struggle and do things he didn't want to, let alone do for me. He is not alone. Many men believe their wives' duty is to take care of them without much reciprocation. I remember hearing him lament to someone that I had taken a couple of hours on a Saturday to get my nails done. I didn't go every week, not even every two weeks, and I never visited a salon or a spa the way I was accustomed to before we met, but something about getting my nails done was just over the top in his estimation. He isn't alone.

My parents reflect this paradigm. Watching my mother prepare three square meals per day for my father, clean and barely get a moment off her feet while he tinkers here and there or piddles with Sudoku simply because his retirement check is larger or because that is her role, really works on my last nerve. I had to admit to myself that watching this behavior modeled before me as a child and into adulthood is likely why I was lousy at selecting a husband.

The status quo, women who aren't supported or encouraged to reach for more in their careers, centers someone else, not you, my sister. Walking into your power at work requires some adjustments at home, and I'm always so pleasantly relieved to get messages and words from husbands who thank me for supporting their wives in their quests. These are women with small and grown children, who are no doubt prioritizing family while they soar, and it's that support at home that gives them the confidence to "keep on moving, don't stop." These women have alignment at home, and that is no doubt the wind beneath their wings.

One time, when I held a challenge with a group of about 20 professional men and women when launching my life coaching practice called The SHIFT™ Coaching, a new mother, a director in a demanding role at a tech company shared her "win or grin" at the top of the call. She had only been able to make one other session, and her breakthrough happened in a very unexpected way. In a conversation about what participants would consider letting go of in order to regain their peace, she had decided to discard her dream to return to school. She told her husband, who promptly told her, "Were you listening on that call with the coach?" Let's have a talk because I don't believe you need to let go of that dream. If I have anything to do with it, you will go get that degree. We just need to talk about how I can support you in making that happen."

The entire group on the call gasped. In fact, someone shouted like they were in church. It was just the testimony we all needed to hear. That shift in mindset had not only caused this incredible woman to think, but a husband, who was tuned in to what she was attempting to do, became an instantaneous, supportive sounding board. She told the group that it was the most productive conversation she and her husband had ever had about the direction of their family during their marriage."

When your partnership is aligned with the same values, you have power, harmony and progress! No threats here. No one is counting your bag against you. This is a very good time to share another secret to your happiness and ability to thrive in an exclusive corporate culture: *Who you partner with* **matters**. It will either derail you, cause you to delay your goals, or, even worse, trample your spirit all at once. We'll explore this more in the next chapter.

There are many more well-documented reasons why women don't ask for what we believe we deserve when it comes to compensation, titles and opportunities. Among them, we doubt our abilities more than men do. We don't want to cause too much trouble, or we believe the company should already see our value and we shouldn't have to state the obvious.

Starstruck by titles, sometimes we overlook the finer details.

One of my college roommates and sorority sisters is now a senior vice president and chief nursing officer in one of the largest hospital systems in the nation. She began her career in nursing after serving in the military, and it didn't come without a struggle. She clearly recalls one of her jumps to senior executive leadership. Making it to that point required an MBA, a doctorate and several certifications, plus years of specialized experience. It also necessitated yet another move across the country.

"When I moved from Colorado to Hawaii, it was such a huge jump from where I was that I didn't even think to question where I fell on the salary band," said Dr. Kecia M. Kelly. "I never even questioned it. I didn't even see it coming."

In fact, she had been in her post for nearly six months when she sought pay adjustments for her direct reports. It was important to her to always seek pay equity – for everyone else. Much to her surprise, her boss delivered, not only for her reports but also for her.

"He just hands me this piece of paper, and he just says, 'I've gotten you a payroll adjustment to get you within market with the other CNOs within [the company],' she recalled. "I looked at it, and it was $50,000."

It was enough to place her in a completely different tax bracket. She got a salary bump that day, but then it hit her; she'd been $50,000 underpaid and never thought to question her original offer.

"I was angry." Dr. Kelly said. "I was angry with myself, and I was angry at them. I was angry at myself for not having a questioning attitude about that salary and not knowing."

Later, she decided to give herself a break because she said she just didn't know or have the mentorship at the time to advise her.

"You don't know what you don't know," she said. But she carried that lesson with her through several subsequent career elevations. Kelly, now at a hospital system in Portland, became fearless about negotiating her worth, and believes she is definitely earning what she deserves, including perks.

Coaching Questions

What new questions will you ask when approached with a new offer or opportunity that you haven't asked in the past?

_____
_____
_____
_____
_____
_____
_____
_____
_____
_____
_____
_____
_____
_____
_____
_____
_____
_____
_____
_____
_____
_____

What is your market value, and how will you find that out?

What other perks can the organization offer you that you never considered before?

What is your vision for your life, and how do you want your next opportunity to support that vision?

What do you need to say to yourself to know that asking for the best title and the best compensation is something that you deserve?

5 AFFIRMATION #4

"I DESERVE A PARTNER WHO RESPECTS, LOVES, AND ADVOCATES FOR ME AND MY LEADERSHIP ASPIRATIONS."

Secret: Your choice of partner will determine if you get to the C-Suite, and your journey might be a lonely one. So, be prepared.

Of all the episodes of the popular 1990s HBO series *Sex in the City*, the one I remember the most, no the one that haunts me the most, is where Miranda Hobbs, the successful power attorney, decides to step up her dating life in search of a partner by doing some speed dating. Long before online dating became more socially acceptable or accessible, Miranda was convinced she needed to put herself out there more to attract the right man. Along with speed dating, she made the choice to dumb down her title to one that men would more readily accept. In fact, she would flat-out lie about what she did for a living. Suddenly, Ms. Hobbs, Esquire, became Miranda, the breathy, high-pitched-voice flight attendant. Her reason being that the minute men learned that she was an attorney, that she had a brain, they would exit stage left. So, she hedged her bets by becoming a woman she barely knew, kicking her authentic self to the curb.

In the beginning, it seemed to work. She increased the number of men who showed interest in her because she had an answer that seemed to be more attractive to them. Mind you, she never questioned why their second question was, "What do you do for a living?" She just wanted to get past that question. The show follows along as one guy falls for her quickly. Before you knew it, the scene had escalated from dinner and drinks to the bedroom. She thought she had found her guy. However, one morning, when she fumbled to share her flight schedule with him, she discovered something didn't quite add up about his story either. He actually worked in retail and wasn't the high-powered corporate titan he led her to believe.

The way this episode was resolved was far from satisfying. The writers led me to believe they were about to have one of the most necessary conversations about women in corporate America and their personal lives. Instead, they took the politically correct way out, and aimed for "both-sidesism."

Lying about who we are is what we all do, men and women. But there is something significant about the fact that some men don't like to date, couple up, or marry women who are smart, ambitious and rewarded for it at work, especially in high-powered spaces. And if these particular men do form a relationship with such a woman, there's a thought that it should be in proper proportion to what they are doing and how much they are making.

That *Sex in the City* episode aired in the late 90s. It's 2023, and conversations about women who aspire to be leaders in business are still less desirable, at least to the most vocal men in the social sphere. In fact, the term "boss babe" has been appropriated by male podcasters who center their content on relationship talk. These men spew the term with the same disdain as extremists on the right who nearly spit each time they use the word "woke."

Is it possible to be a successful woman in corporate America and have a supportive, loving and respectful partner who doesn't feel emasculated or undermined by the mere thought of it? It absolutely is, and yet, it absolutely isn't. Anecdotally, I know who these C-Suite women are and their husbands, but the statistics show something else.

Who you choose as a partner can boost your ability to make it to the highest levels of leadership, or it can completely sabotage it. A 2023 study from Pew Research uncovered that even when women out-earn their spouses, they still do the majority of the housework. And as women trend upward in earnings, their leisure time is still diminished while men's leisure increases.

A 2020 article in *Fast Company* had a headline that grabbed my attention, but it didn't surprise me. It was called "Why ambitious women get divorced more than ambitious men." The stat that grounded the write-up was telling: "Women who become CEOs are more than twice as likely to get divorced within three years as their male counterparts." The article goes on to tell the stories of five different executive women and their experiences in marriage, dating and divorce as a direct result of having leadership aspirations. While I don't know those women personally, I certainly know others with similar stories, and it is pretty clear that I've also lived out all three scenarios. I've also observed the good, the bad and the otherwise questionable while dating.

However, recently, I was pleasantly surprised when a man reached out to me on LinkedIn to thank me for the support that I was giving his wife. I had no clue that these two were connected, let alone married, but they both connected with me on the career platform, and she was enrolled in a mastermind that I was hosting on regaining one's peace and productivity. I cannot tell you the joy that overflowed, and it was simply because this husband wanted to see his wife succeed in leadership and reach for more than she was currently. It was so much so that he was motivated to reach out to me and let me know.

Comparatively, the data and anecdotes from that *Fast Company* article about marriages that go south on high-powered women in corporate reveals that this husband was indeed a unicorn. However, several of those unicorns have galloped by in my practice and made themselves known one way or the other. In a couple of cases, these were not only husbands, they were fathers, even of newborns.

Although my experience with marriage and dating has been far from awesome, I'm aware that high-powered women can and do find partners who are not only supportive but all in.

When Anne Chow was appointed the first woman of color CEO of an AT&T business unit in the company's 144-year history, the media coverage ensued. Profile after profile exploded from the press because this Asian-American woman seemed to have accomplished the impossible. But the subscript of her story wasn't simply about her leadership, commitment to excellence, diversity, equity and inclusion. Instead, another theme emerged. Beyond her Juilliard training as a classical pianist, some writers uncovered how she did it all and where she found support at home. Anne's 25-year marriage to her husband, Bob Moore, was important to the narrative. She would now be at the helm of a $37 billion global business, and her husband seemed to be all in. But that began years before this historic appointment. Multiple sources reported that Moore was a stay-at-home husband. Traditional roles had been switched. When both of their girls were young, the couple made the decision that he would proactively retire early, aged just 39, after an 18-year career in IT.

Anne and I reconnected recently to discuss how that one decision removed a tremendous load off her mentally and emotionally so that she could excel in the executive ranks of leadership. She admits that she wouldn't have done well at home or at work had she tried to split her time.

"I credit him as the one who helped me manage our priorities and my stress from the standpoint of we knew we wanted to have children, and we also knew that we did not want to outsource parenting," Chow said. "And so you imagine one of the biggest pressures that working moms face is that pressure of how do I parent well and have a successful career at the same time when I feel so often that I'm doing neither. Because I'm not dedicated to either full-time, whether it's in body, spirit, heart, or mind, right?

"And so, for me, the fact that my husband stepped up to take on the primary caregiver role fairly early on in our children's lives was a huge blessing and a huge worry off of my shoulders because I knew that they had a parent who could be fully present at all times. And that was something that I absolutely, absolutely needed for my own peace of mind."

Chow said that this decision, which was one of a number that she and Bob made early in their relationship, was absolutely one that secured their happiness, in combination with the fact that she enjoyed her career more and likely showed the most earning potential.

"The decision that we made 100% is related to our strength, security and happiness as a family. Why? Because it was anchored in a mutual decision, a mutual shared set of values, a mutual shared set of priorities and a commitment to our family and our children that these were the roles that we were to play," Chow said.

And while she agreed that financial security can indeed help you find happiness, the decision for Bob to stay with the kids and manage the home did come with its social pressures and backlash. In settings with other parents, and even with family members, the awkward questions and comments ensued.

"We had friends and acquaintances who liked to make side jabs. Such as saying, hey, what do you do all day? Sit around eating bonbons?" Chow said. "Those comments would come from men, by the way. Not women, because inherently, women know that parenting and being the primary caregiver is incredibly hard work. I've always said that Bob has had the harder job between the two of us. And I absolutely believe it. He also had the more important job. Actually, *the* most important job."

Then other men, friends, husbands, and fathers were more genuine and admitted their perceived limitations, albeit mostly a preference and sometimes bias, not to do this work of becoming the primary caregiver.

"We had *many* of our closest friends where the husband, the father figure, openly admitted that they couldn't do it," Chow said. "They'd often cite that it was their job to be the breadwinner and they just couldn't see themselves at home full time. As for me, I feel very, very, very lucky that Bob never felt that way. And I've appreciated all that he's done and continues to do for our family."

Anne's most proud of the results their decision yielded – highly empathetic, smart, kind and responsible daughters who now have a less conventional way of looking at women, women leaders, men and the roles they can play in the family dynamic to reach mutual goals.

"Our daughters have a point of view developed by first-hand experiences about what being a mom and being a female leader is all about," she said. "They have a point of view about dads. They have a very special relationship with their father, and there is no traditional anything in their eyes. They've grown up with this idea that if you want a life partner, you deserve a life partner who wants the same dreams that you have and is willing to take part in doing that. And that it requires mutual sacrifice, trust and compromise, and a true partnership."

Anne's husband, Bob, is a great example of the kind of men who are willing to work with aspiring women leaders. And it isn't simply about his willingness to take on the household. It is deeper than that, and there are other meaningful traits that high-performing women can look for before committing that could very well put them on the right track for a successful partnership as they reach for the highest levels of leadership; qualities such as kindness, generosity, and as Anne emphasized again and again, *selflessness*.

She offered this advice to women newly dating for partnership or perhaps even on their second or third go around.

Have important conversations early.

Discuss values early in the dating relationship and get to the details, including faith, finances, family and even political leanings that could clash later in the marriage. She mentioned that it isn't enough to talk about whether or not you want to have children; instead, it should be about how you want to raise the children. Which of you will take primary responsibility for doing that, and what sacrifices will either of you make to make it happen? When it comes to faith, she says that whether or not you share the same religion, you must find out if you are grounded in the same values that drive your faith. And as for finances, go beyond mere conversations about spending and saving habits to the living standards you aspire to. Discussing how money will be made between the two of you, who will make that money, and the importance of how much you make, spend and save is paramount.

The story of Bob and Anne is a good one to map out how it could work in a non-traditional way. It forces some hard questions and discussions, whatever the route you take, including identifying the cautionary traits in a mate for aspiring women leaders.

Is your potential partner enamored with or stuck in traditional models of partnership?

When identifying the traits of the most ideal partners for women leaders with C-Suite aspirations, the willingness to re-think and, in some cases, completely deconstruct or do away with the idea of "roles" is paramount. And it has been amazing to me to uncover that a good number of men, especially Black men, who are dating for marriage or long-term partnerships, resist the idea, at least anecdotally, even if at first they seem to be on board. This throwback mindset can be revealed in some seemingly small points of view. For instance, the push-pull that happened in my home about whether to hire a housekeeper when I was married. But what I've found about my mother's generation is that they cleaned out of necessity and didn't have these high-octane careers that many Black women and other women of color have today. When I asked my nearly 80-year-old mother whether, given the access, opportunity, and means to hire a housekeeper when my sister and I were younger, she would have done so, her response was an unequivocal yes!

So, must being married be an agreement to step back in time and live the lives our mothers lived because someone else in the house benefits from it? This, again, is cultural. Men who were raised in households that never saw a different narrative for their mothers tend to transfer that onto their girlfriends and wives. So it's important to understand what was modeled before them as boys to understand what you are facing with them as men.

For many women, their C-Suite aspirations happen after they've already chosen their life partners. In other words, they married their partner, and then their desires evolved, shifted or were revealed. Consequently, they find themselves needing to retrofit. This creates conflict.

Is he competitive with you?

There is nothing worse than a life partner or romantic interest who constantly pits himself against you or compares himself to you. Friendships can be destroyed over less. Competitiveness can reveal itself in obvious or less obvious ways. Does he compare compensation or projects or even how you went about solving a problem? Sometimes these partners will silence you when speaking about ideas, happenings or projects that excite you.

I remember dating a man I thought would be a great candidate for a highly driven woman because he himself was a VP at a company. However, whenever I tried to talk to him about an opportunity with a well-known organization that had some high-profile players involved, he would tell me to stop talking about the opportunity. I thought he'd be a great sounding board, but this wasn't the conversation he wanted to have with the woman he was seeing. Instead, he'd rather discuss what was for dinner and what craft beer he wanted with the Delmonico he loved for me to prepare. That steak was definitely perfect, but I'll never cook again for a man who requires me to shrink.

At some point, I started eliminating men who, within the first couple of conversations, made a big deal over whether I could cook or not. I love cooking, and I'm rather good at it. I find preparing cuisines from around the globe not only fun, but I love to do it, and my family and friends rave over it. I consider myself to be a foodie and have the guidance of my ancestors because I don't follow cookbooks or measure unless I'm baking. But the minute a man starts pushing to know if I can cook, I either wrap things and move on or I immediately ask them if they can cook. The reality is that these days, I rarely cook. Indeed, I tried a meal service while starting the search for a personal chef just this year. My focus is on other things, and managing a man's expectations about this early on is important.

Is he controlling?

Once I made friends with a man who was married. Our conversations were largely around business because a mutual contact introduced us. At some point, I became friends with his wife. I would learn more about how their household worked from multiple interactions with her. She used to have a corporate job, but at some point she stopped and became a full-time housewife. I would learn as the days went by that while she was shouldering all of the housework, including cooking, cleaning and childcare, she was bored out of her mind. She had a seedling of a business that she hadn't nurtured, so I encouraged her to work on that to curb the boredom.

Shortly thereafter, she started to pull away, and neither one of them provided any insight into why the change happened. However, over time, as I spoke with him about various topics, his determination to control the narrative in his home began to spill over into our conversation regarding seemingly unrelated topics, like how he believed traditional roles for women and men in marriage weren't patriarchal, and how happiness as a part of marriage wasn't really what anyone is actually signing up for.

His wife had begun to talk to me about the possibility of engaging my services to get her life organized and on track, but all of that talk stopped. In fact, gradually, I found I had zero access to her. She stopped returning benign text messages. Her husband had successfully controlled the situation. I was the walking embodiment of an empowered woman, and while he would continue to try to have conversations with me about my work, which I soon began to shut down, apparently, these were not conversations he wanted me to have with his wife.

What are you looking for in a mate, then?

Here are other questions to ask about the person you are dating or with whom you are considering a life-long commitment:

- » Can he share or yield the limelight when it is your time to shine?
- » Can he celebrate your wins when there is no benefit to him?
- » Is he comfortable in his own skin?
- » Does he have respect in his field, with his family and his community, and a solid reputation as someone with character?
- » Does he have a growth mindset?
- » How were marriage and roles modeled for him growing up, and how much of that still informs his thinking?

Meet the mate women leaders who want to ascend should avoid at all costs.

Let's get clear on this persona, this archetype. This man is well-packaged. By any sense of the word, he is seen as a good guy in his circles but nothing deeper than that. His work is very important to him. He centers family, community and even his culture. Spiritually, he is either committed to his faith or calls himself spiritual. He obtained his undergraduate degree and sometimes even has an advanced degree. He most likely grew up in church, and sometimes he is still very much involved in church ministry. If he isn't, he is definitely engaged with his fraternity or Masons, whether that is volunteerism or simply supporting and socializing with his line brothers or friends from college. This is important to him. He seems to be very dedicated to his mother. In fact, in some cases, they seem a tad too close, and she keeps his secrets. He is well-spoken, easy on the eyes and seems to have the ability to charm anyone who comes into contact with him. He's introverted or extroverted but very concerned about appearances and how he is perceived.

When it comes to his spouse, he married very well. In fact, you may even say he married up or will marry up, but don't say that to him. He snagged that beautiful Black woman we've all come to know in the stats. She is over-credentialed with more advanced degrees than any other group. She is a superstar at work and may even have a successful small business. She is active in community organizations, most often leading them. She is on the rise, but also very dedicated to her family, frequently denying herself in favor of her children and husband. She is not good at "me time." Both she and her husband paid close attention to the way their parents modeled family in the household and the roles they adopted. Her mother never really took "me time" outside of possibly getting her hair done, but in Black culture, that's a duty, not a frill.

Conflict arises when she mentions how overly tired she is, but not in the way you would think. He is always very open to any conversation about her peeling back on her career work, even quitting, but not necessarily as open with regard to housework, cooking or other domestic tasks. Having a housekeeper, a nanny or a personal chef is a sore spot topic for the two of them. After all, he never saw his mother hire out or outsource. He watched his mother come home and prepare meals in time for his father to come home from work and plop on the sofa to watch the evening news and retire in the evening, if he was even present in the home. For some, they watched their mothers do everything and become run down and exhausted all the time. If anyone was catered to, it was him.

They say that you can't be it if you can't see it, and this is where the idea of a woman carrying most, if not all, of the emotional and physical labor in the household (without perhaps the taking out of the trash or yard work) becomes a generational issue for this kind of man. They've never seen a woman in their home be a boss, so they don't have any paradigm to refer to. In fact, the support at home, like personal chefs, nannies, tutors, housekeepers, household managers and the like, in his mind, are reserved for the rich. He has no understanding that outsourcing work like this is actually how these wealthy leaders *became* rich. To him, it doesn't compute that you have to spend money to make money or that you need to have this sort of support to focus on the things that make you money. He suffers from a fixed mindset. It's also a scarcity mindset, and, unfortunately, our partners can bring this thinking into our homes and absolutely destroy any desire or possibility of becoming the leaders that women, and for that matter, even *they* could become.

This mindset keeps this man's partner tethered as if in shackles. It is the man that says working hard is the way to wealth and freedom. When working hard keeps you exhausted and, well, working *hard* simply to maintain. There is no freedom in it, and if there is, you're too exhausted to experience it.

He needs to believe that you can do more by doing less

The idea of working more and harder is what keeps people in a lower tax bracket. It's a mindset that believes that making $120K allows you to say you make six figures, and that that in itself is an achievement. It's unfocused and will weigh heavily on your mental and physical health.

What if I told you that you could make seven figures by doing less? When exploring ways to be more productive with my clients, I ask them how they might recuperate their time. I share with them the simple and effective coaching tool of the 4Ds when looking at the many things on their plate. I challenge them to ask these simple questions when considering a list of tasks:

- » How can I *delay* it?
- » What might I do to *delegate* it (with people, processes, or automation)?
- » What would make it possible to *delete* it?
- » What makes this important enough for me to *do* it?

Challenging my clients to be the masters of their time is important. After all, whatever is in charge of your time, rules your life. Therefore, applying the rule of the 4Ds to your calendar and prioritizing the important over the urgent is paramount. The way forward is to focus on the things that will accelerate you toward freedom and the life to which you aspire. It is a different reality from those who limit their future to how they worked in the past. They've worked in positions where supervisors, managers or someone else was in charge of their time. So that is how they approach their work and their life.

Culturally, women, people of color and most of the middle class and less advantaged live in the construct where someone else is in charge, not themselves. We have been conditioned to exist and be content in subordinate roles, to be the workhorses. So being the masters of our time is a relatively foreign concept to us. So we typically defer to someone when it comes to planning, and we expect to do the work of that plan. We watched our parents work their fingers to the bone and listened to our grandparents and great-grandparents tell stories of struggle. All of it was extrinsically motivated.

For example, consider this statement: "I have to pay my car note because someone will repossess my car if I do not." Or, "I must get home from work before a certain time because my husband will be looking for me and want dinner." The thought is this: If I don't do X, Y will happen to me. And someone else has expectations, and I'm living in *fear*. You cannot dream when you are afraid. Fear dashes hope. Hope is a prerequisite for dreaming. Dreams are required to set goals. The only thought for those living in fear is making it, surviving by ensuring someone else is satisfied with whatever they do so they can simply exist. People like this have a scarcity mindset, believing that resources are scarce. Often, they are concerned that someone with more power is in charge of those resources, like their time, their money, and ultimately their fate and future. It is the eternal state of dependency. Essentially accepting that the only thing to look forward to is some form of punishment or sanction if you don't get something done that is expected of you.

Spending money to make money is terrifying to someone with a scarcity mindset, and these individuals may simply have a hard time wrapping their heads around it, let alone accepting it. Raising the idea that you want to pay someone for support around the house with someone with a scarcity mindset may trigger anything from a lively debate to an all-out battle.

I watched my mother do it all alone: cooking three square meals a day, combing and pressing my hair and that of my sister, doing most of the housework inside the home, working a full-time job as a teacher (which requires that you bring work home with you), and she still managed to look amazing on Sundays when it was time for church. I'm not sure how she did it, and looking back, she isn't quite sure either. But she will say it was with the help of the Lord.

I purchased my first home as a single woman in my mid-twenties. It was a starter home by any standards, but it was all mine. I worked a 60-hour work week, so there were two things that I decided to make permanent in my budget: grocery delivery and a bi-weekly housekeeper. Not even four years later, I was up for a VP role, and I wasn't yet 30. During that time, I was on a flight twice weekly, and I loved to come home to an uncluttered home and freshly mopped floors. My mother, or my father for that matter, never once questioned or chided my choices. In fact, my mother said she understood. It stoked pride in my father that I had this kind of career and control over my life. After all, I was working for a global company. I had huge responsibilities that kept me tethered to my pager or smart device nights and weekends. And although I was single and had no children, my parents, despite the fact that they came up in a different time, saw the housekeeper and grocery delivery as must-haves.

Your faith may have you conflicted about what it means to be a good wife, but it shouldn't.

Just recently, my mother told me that while she was reading a book I gave her for Christmas, called *Kingdom Woman,* written by my pastor and his eldest daughter, she was reminded of me. She recalled a story of how my pastor noticed how his daughter was struggling to homeschool five children and run a business and ministry while still being an attentive wife. So he offered to get her support until she and her husband could afford it. That story made my mother think of a statement I made about how some men today, with so-called "traditional values," blame their misogyny on their faith, pointing to Proverbs 31 as the model of a virtuous woman. She said to me that these men don't understand that famous chapter. That the woman in that scripture wasn't described as industrious because she was keeping the house. She was also a woman of enterprise outside of the home. Being the Bible scholar that my mother is, she recalled that even the women of little means back then had handmaidens, nurses, midwives, housekeepers and other forms of help around the home. That having help around the house was not reserved for the wealthy. In fact, in verse 15, the scripture notes that she brings "portions for her female servants." Note the plural. That statement also implies that she may also have male servants too. It mentions that she buys land and invests with her earnings. *Earnings.* The Proverbs 31 woman works outside of the home and is likely a businesswoman because *she had income.* "She sees that her trading is profitable." And later, it says that she ensures that she receives a good price for her sales. The most fascinating part of the chapter reveals that she *manages* the affairs of her household. This could mean that whether there were nannies, housekeepers, yard workers, or nurses, *she was in charge of how the house was run,* not necessarily involved in the housework herself. This kind of woman was special, according to the Bible. So it makes perfect sense that she didn't marry just anyone. The scripture describes her husband as a respected member of the city, "where he takes his seat among the elders in the land." This husband is no slouch. The word implies that he is wise and has a stellar reputation in his community.

Many of the men who demand that their wives bear the brunt of domestic work while working outside of the home (or, for that matter, even as stay-at-home wives) haven't made it to the stature of the Proverbs 31 man.

Sit with that.

The other reason why Black women are spewing from the middle of the leadership pipeline

I listened to that stay-at-home wife I mentioned earlier tell me that when she was worn down from her last job, it was so bad that she needed therapy. So when her husband suggested she leave the workforce, she jumped at it. The irony is that she was *still working,* and possibly harder than she was outside of the home. She started homeschooling her children, whom she admitted could be more than a handful, while still taking on the lion's share of the housework and cooking. She was now overworked and not paid for it. Sure, her former work environment was toxic, but this intelligent sister needed another outlet to exercise her business mind and skills.

Did they ever discuss her finding another job? I guess I will never know. Being a stay-at-home wife sounded good at first, but four years in, she told me that she was bored and felt like she wasn't doing anything (but she used an expletive). I felt her pain. She had the makings of a business that she wanted to grow, but she was too exhausted and bogged down with the work of the house to work on it the way she wanted.

I was intrigued, but not shocked, that the option her husband provided her when she expressed her stress and anxiety years before was to quit working outside the home altogether. I never heard her say that getting help with the work at home was an option. With their income, from what I could tell, they could afford tutors, nannies, housekeepers and chefs if they wanted, but those options didn't seem to be on the table. That's when it dawned on me. The current arrangement *benefited him*. Three years into the pandemic, and he was still working from home. He was living the high life while his wife was struggling, and a job in corporate America had nothing to do with it.

Why wasn't I surprised? My ex-husband also raised the idea of me exiting the job market about the time that I was expecting my daughter. I considered it, but before I could make a decision on my own, I was laid off from the job that paid what he called "entirely too much money." So, I settled into the idea of taking a break and doing some light consulting. Two months later, I received an offer

I couldn't refuse, working for the big company where I'd learn so much, and my life would change.

So, I had a close call with exiting the workforce because of a spouse who wanted me home despite my storied expertise and experiences, dual degrees and a passion so deep that I ran an agency for nearly a decade. But I suppose stimulating my brain and interests just wasn't an item on his agenda. And I hear that this is the case for many women leaders with dating prospects, serious relationships and even marriages.

This scenario is yet another example of women who are no longer in the leadership pipeline. Those who left mid-career, not because someone pushed them out from an organization, but due to an overpowering influencer in their own homes who pulled them out.

You deserve a partner with an abundance mindset and an unselfish, empathetic heart

Stephen Covey wrote about the concept of the scarcity and abundance mindsets. He first introduced them in his best-selling book *7 Habits of Highly Successful People*. It is fair to say, however, that some people confuse the idea of appearing to have abundance, or even accumulating material things, with having an abundance mindset. You can have plenty of things but still have a scarcity mindset. An abundance mindset is what is necessary when attempting to change your life and reach for audacious leadership goals. If you believe in abundance and the notion that there are plenty of resources for everyone, but your partner does not, it can spell conflict that results in disastrous outcomes – emotionally and financially. It can even affect your children.

***

COACHING QUESTIONS

How will you approach dating and marriage differently now that you are clear on the importance of a supportive partnership?

_____
_____
_____
_____
_____
_____
_____
_____
_____
_____
_____
_____
_____
_____
_____
_____
_____
_____
_____
_____
_____

What are some of the issues that are sticking points for you and your partner or whomever you may be involved with?

_____
_____
_____
_____
_____
_____
_____
_____
_____
_____
_____
_____
_____
_____
_____
_____
_____
_____
_____
_____
_____
_____
_____
_____
_____

If you are married, how will you begin to address issues that may be holding you back from your leadership aspirations?

_____
_____
_____
_____
_____
_____
_____
_____
_____
_____
_____
_____
_____
_____
_____
_____
_____
_____
_____
_____
_____
_____
_____
_____

What old ways of thinking might you need to let go of at home as a woman leader?

What behavior shifts might you make that will improve your dating, relationship or marriage, keeping your leadership aspirations in mind

What tough conversations do you need to have with your partner that might clear the path for your aspirations and your combined aspirations?

6 AFFIRMATION #5

"I DESERVE TO BE HAPPY, SAFE, AND WHOLE ON MY LEADERSHIP JOURNEY."

Secret: Reaching your leadership potential will be difficult if you aren't happy.

You've heard of the Old Black Tax, right? It's the idea that you must work at least twice as hard and be twice as good as your white counterparts to obtain or keep a job. Whatever ancestor created the concept was right to call it a tax because not only is it extra, it wears on you. It is literally taxing. I can't even remember the first time my parents told me this, but I had to be in high school or college. It was a way to say that I shouldn't give them any reason to discredit me, so that if they do, it clearly isn't about the work, whether school work or professional.

That is a heavy burden to live with as a young person, but I really didn't feel the pressure of it until I was well into my professional life.

When I was in grade school, I attended a Christian academy in the middle of Oak Cliff, a subdivision of Dallas, which is about half the city's landmass. Some consider it the "South Side," the same way one might reference the less empowered part of another city like Chicago. But the truth is there was plenty of old money in Oak Cliff, and still is. Most of the old money is white, and they didn't leave when white flight happened in the 1960s and 70s. The majority of Oak Cliff was then, as now, considerably Black and brown. Now that my classmates and I are adults, we look back and are proud to say that in a school, even a private one that was more than 50% Black and brown, we were doing diversity and inclusion long before those words were even "a thing"-- and doing it well. I know that it is shocking to hear these days because many of today's Christian academies have a totally different agenda, and many of these organizations are not shy about saying so. At my school, no one took a second glance at interracial couples walking down the down halls hand-in-hand, arm-in-arm or even "hugged up." These couples came in all varieties too. Most of the faculty and staff were white, but we had some very strong Latino and Black teachers who we all admired. The parents were great too. Mind you, there were less than 300 of us in the entire high school, at its peak, so everyone felt like family and acted like it too.

We had psychological safety before we even knew what that was, until, that is, we left campus to compete in sports. There was always some other school where the students and even some parents were determined to remind us that *this* school from *that* part of town, with the championship basketball team, was different, but not in a good way. You see, our three-time state championship team had all Black players and just one white player (who, at the time, probably had no clue that he was). The other schools typically had the reverse. The reminders that we were different came in the form of taunting chants, sometimes referees who piled on bogus calls, and once or twice, someone slashed the tires on our school bus.

As I look for the good in situations, I have determined that those experiences prepared me for what was next in college life. My time at Texas Christian University absolutely prepared me for what I'd eventually face as a professional.

Those experiences at university would have gone undocumented had I not been writing about them in my weekly column in the daily school newspaper, at least most of them. I didn't write about the one experience that would cause me to quit the cheer squad in my senior year, skip out on related yearbook pictures and any other on-campus activities. I longed to graduate and get on with "real life," as I would put it. At least, I thought that story would be undocumented. But then I was approached by a

Ph.D. at the university in 2021 to be a part of TCU's Race & Reconciliation Initiative's oral history project.

The story that I shared concerned the 1992 Homecoming Queen election. But what was more important than the story itself was the absolute cathartic and therapeutic experience I had telling it for the first time, out loud to someone who was not my close family. And it wasn't simply the telling of it. It was the fact that someone acknowledged that my story, the way I experienced it, needed to be told, validated and somehow reconciled.

The invitation was almost unimaginable, and I surprised myself during the interview as well. As many times as I go on camera and share stories of inequities, whether mine, my sisters of color, or someone else's, those tales never once brought me to tears like this one. Even the recounting of my experience at the big company where I was systematically removed for no other reason than my new white bosses thought I needed to be reigned in, and instead used a Hispanic woman and Black man to get the job done.

You see, typically, Black people take stories of discrimination, racism and hurt to their graves because no one acknowledges them, validates them or reconciles them. I realized as I spoke to the PhD who interviewed me, that those wounds were still fresh, nearly 30 years later. They were fresh because no one had addressed them, and I had suppressed them.

At this point, you may be wondering why I haven't shared the story here. The story is public record as a part of the oral history. The university has posted it to its website, and I've even told portions of the story on social media. But for the purposes of this book, the most important aspect of the story is that I had a chance to begin to really heal. You see, oftentimes, we believe that we have healed simply because we escaped the situation and moved on. However, as Black women and other women of color, we often carry that trauma right into the next chapter of our lives. I know that I did, and it colored almost every experience I would have regarding race from that day forward. It wasn't until I was sitting before the oral history project facilitator, crying so much that they stopped the camera, that I realized that this was truly the healing moment my university and I both needed.

You wouldn't have known it from the 50 giant billboards, 30 bus panels and national television ads where the university featured my smiling face for their huge TCU Lead On advertising campaign between 2015-2018. It was history-making. I was the first Black student or faculty member to be a part of the campaign, and it wasn't the first time I'd made history at the school. As I look back on my college story and how it impacted the rest of my adult life, I see the similarities between what most women of color have endured.

Grin, bear it, and keep it pushing

We must learn to slow down enough to process and heal to reclaim our happiness.

When I meet with my female clients, I note the similarities in experiences between them. The gender issues are steady, but I notice a spike in other biases when I speak to women of color, especially Black women leaders. Their stories are so alike. Sometimes, the only difference is the name, perhaps the organization they work for, or the part of the country they are from. Not only are their stories strikingly similar, but so are the ways they tend to handle the situations where they are minimized, left out, pushed out, disrespected, cheated or passed over. She toughens up. She moves on to the next opportunity, but she never really allows herself to process what has happened to her. There's usually no time for that, she surmises. She's simply happy to be out of the situation.

I didn't realize how this cycle had so impacted me until I was sitting with my therapist discussing personal and relationship issues. She asked me a simple question: "How did that make you feel?" It's a question I've begun to ask my clients because it is powerful. My response was not what she expected. I did not know how to express my feelings with words that were actually "feeling" words. I would answer with statements like, "I felt betrayed," or "I felt belittled." She stopped me and said, "But those are words that describe someone else's actions toward you." I was stumped. I didn't know what words to use. So she gave me a sheet with all sorts of feeling words like, sad, glad, mad, worried, afraid, happy. Looking at the page, it all seemed so simple, so why didn't I know how to use those words?

My assignment from the therapist was to go home and practice using these words at the moment that I was feeling the emotions. I was stunned to note how absolutely difficult it was, but eventually, I learned.

As I began to understand more about neuroscience research and how our brains work, it hit me that this is learned behavior. Obviously, I'd practiced this cycle again and again: experience hurt, pick myself up, press down the hurt, talk about it in terms of what someone else did to hurt me, remain positive, because my dad said so, and then move on and try to avoid the same hurt next time. This pattern isn't simply about work. This is about life, and I'd have to unlearn the pattern by repeating healthier behavior.

That page from my therapist would take me through the next several years of my life until I was okay saying out loud how I felt and describing those feelings with accuracy and preciseness.

Years later, in my own coaching practice, I met high-achieving Black women leader after leader who suffered from the same emotional challenge. They simply didn't know how to express how they felt with words that described their true feelings. Although my therapist was a white woman, she said she had seen it before too, but mainly with high-achieving Black women. She surmised that perhaps it was indeed cultural that we found ourselves in situations where, when we were hurt, we'd immediately pick ourselves up and move on without allowing ourselves to process it. Perhaps it was out of necessity, maybe even survival, or maybe it was what we saw our mothers do.

Dorinda Walker, CEO of the Cultural Solutions Group, recalls being quietly demoted from a previous company role despite delivering outstanding results year after year and winning repeated awards. Once she published a book recounting her personal triumphs over drugs and abuse, the accolades and requests to speak began to multiply. She recalls that once she began to shine "too much," her boss put her in another part of the business where the work was slower, and she could ultimately have less impact. She was bored and belittled.

"The realization came to me because I was coming to work miserable, not liking what I was doing, and I felt like I was starting over," she said. "I was going into rooms having to educate a room full of non-people of color about why culture and diversity matters. And I felt like I was doing that my whole career. I don't want to start over."

Dorinda was done. She said God spoke to her, and she decided at that moment to do what the U.S. Census says so many Black women resort to when they decide to leave corporate – start her own business. In 2017, Catalyst told us why, explaining that Black women are fed up with being treated this way in corporate America.

More recently, the pandemic only added gasoline to the blaze. According to a 2020 report from the U.S. Department of Labor, Black women displayed the biggest decline in the workforce compared to any other group. Many of them remained unemployed, but those with more education and corporate experience were starting businesses at a faster clip than their counterparts and other groups. Findings from a recent American Express small business report revealed that between 2014-2019, women-owned businesses grew by 21%, and Black woman-owned businesses by 50%.

Dorinda was a part of that group. She didn't skip a beat. In 2019, she picked herself up, brushed herself off and started her own business, which is a stressful process no matter how you approach it.

We are grieving, but we rarely let it out.

We need to learn to emote so that we can release and move forward in a healthy way.

Another time I wound up on my therapist's couch was after some man ghosted me. It really punched me in the gut, or so I thought. Until, in one session, my therapist observed very insightfully that I hadn't been seeing the man long enough to be as hurt as I appeared to be. Then she reflected back to me everything that had happened to me within four months:

- » I'd been laid off from a job that I really enjoyed. And, while I'd grieved the toxicity of the environment I found myself in a year prior and was thrilled to escape, I was suddenly separated from hundreds of coworkers who I'd liked working with for the past six years.
- » I received news of a friend who committed suicide in a fairly grizzly fashion and was unable to attend the funeral.
- » Although my business was off to a great start, I had started a business single-handedly.

Again, I had not given myself the space to process everything that had happened – the losses in my life, the major shifts, and changing dynamics. That caused the ghosting to hit me with the weight of three losses, far more impact than the true value of the incident to me. I'll admit that penning *No Thanks* shortly thereafter was the therapy and healing I needed, and I didn't stop seeing my therapist during that time either.

If Black women aren't happy in corporate America, it may not be simply because we face stiffer challenges when it comes to bias than our white counterparts. It may also relate to the impact of those challenges, and we don't deal with them properly. We rarely allow ourselves to grieve, process and heal completely. We definitely don't cry at work if we can possibly avoid it because that would feed into the gender-biased trope that women are emotional and out of control. Every woman can agree that crying is the last thing they'd ever want to do on the job.

Dorinda's story is a great example of how her dealing with stress at work differed from how even her boss, who happened to be a white woman, did. Once, after Dorinda returned to the office from her book tour and speaking events, her boss confronted her about her activities. Dorinda said the conversation was so contentious that she took it to human resources. When the exchange was over, Dorinda went to her office, closed the door, and called her mother, who made her laugh. She then moved on. Her boss took the next day off, returned on Monday then knocked on her door seeking closure. She told Dorinda that after their meeting, she went to the ladies' room and threw up. We can only assume that hurl included tears.

Dorinda let her know that she had moved on, and in her words, "I have three children at home. I do not need to babysit another one at work. And I told her to go in her office and get her stuff together, and then when she was ready to work with me as a professional, then we could move on."

It takes practice to stand up for yourself, unwavering in the face of colleagues and bosses who are in one moment coming for you, and the next, following up days later seeking closure, sympathy even, as they process their emotions without regard for how you might feel. They drag out conversations that you are expecting to dissipate, then show up again like Freddie Krueger. They just won't die.

Yes, we take all of this home with us. We rely on our faith to brush off grudges, and we keep it moving.

But is that healthy?

Finding happiness means you must find ways to align with your values and set boundaries.

Dr. Kecia Kelly, a Vice President and Chief Nursing Officer, said she believes that happiness is key to success, but that happiness for her relies on being valued where she works.

"I do think that it's important to be happy, and content, and to feel valued," she said. "I would probably lead with feeling valued because when I haven't felt valued, that's usually when I start moving on to something else. I don't hold anyone responsible for my happiness except me. But I do hold people responsible for valuing me in the workplace and what I have to offer."

A 2022 article in Black Enterprise found that Black women who don't feel valued are simply exhausted with being undervalued because of the emotional toll it takes. Sometimes, that exhaustion is also physical because moving on can, and often does, involve a moving truck. Picking up your life to get to the best possible role in the next step of your career is a major decision. How that impacts your family is also a heavy consideration.

Dr. Kecia Kelly, who now resides in Portland, Oregon, moved many times in her career, amassing three degrees, the highest being a Doctor of Nursing Practice, Executive Leadership. She also has three crucial certifications that she worked on between all the cities, across every part of the United States, including two stints in Hawaii. She says that forming good relationships is difficult because she feels she is never anywhere long enough, and she admits that now that she is in the top tier, it can be lonely at times. However, she says there is a wonderful upside.

"My husband and I are financially comfortable. I can financially support my parents so that they have a comfortable retirement life, and my sons have learned the value of the hustle."

Ultimately, Dr. Kelly has found peace and happiness in that fact, primarily because those results align with her values. It's been what has motivated her all these years, giving back to her mother, who sacrificed so much for her, and modeling a work ethic for her two sons.

Along with tapping into her values, Kecia has found that boundary setting, making a solid contribution in her work and venting to her husband have helped her to maintain her joy when things have gotten tough.

Finding solace in affirming family members and people who can identify with what you're experiencing can help you reclaim happiness.

Leaning into loved ones and inward reflection is crucial.

Isolation is a feeling many Black women experience once they make it to the C-Suite. Emily K. Graham, Chief Equity and Impact Officer at Omnicom, didn't hesitate to share how lonely she felt and exactly when the loneliness might strike.

"When you're walking into that first executive meeting, or the business trip where you have to be away for two or three days, and it's just you, and you have to have countless interactions and dinners and meetings and small discussions," Graham said. "And you wonder when you walk up, are people stopping to talk because I'm outside and I don't belong? And these executives have already created this relationship with one another. So, yeah, there's a lot of that. And the confidence that you build has to first start with you stopping to blame yourself or kick yourself, like doubting, [or thinking] you don't belong here. I know *you do* belong here."

Graham said she managed to clear that hurdle and pulled herself through the discomfort through introspection.

"When you would go on trips or going to meetings and you kind of retreat back and debrief with yourself on how did you do, what points did you make, where they [were] resonant, you know, analyzing the way I do, because that's just kind of a facet of my leadership and my personality."

Graham also relies on her mother, who spent all of her career at a huge corporation.

"She gave me so much perspective, and she had seen and been around quite a bit of being a young, started working at 18, in the seventies," Graham said. "And so I would just call her for affirmation, ask her for guidance, get some perspective, recognize that I'm standing in the shoes and coming from a long lineage of incredibly strong people."

Celebrating other women fosters positive emotion.

We need to sincerely cheer each other on.

While it is indeed important to celebrate our own accomplishments, we shouldn't overlook the impact that celebrating the wins of others can have on our happiness and well-being.

Andrea Williams, chief experience officer at the Utah Jazz, learned this later in her career after feeling somewhat isolated in the male-dominated front offices in the sports industry. Previously the chief operating officer of the College Football Playoff, she learned that celebrating the victories, big and small, of other women became infectious and triggered positive emotions.

"You know, when you're not looking inward, and you're looking outward, and you're projecting positivity, and you're projecting grace and advancement for others, there's joy in that," Williams said. "And once you recognize that you can still be successful, you can still achieve things, but at the same time, recognize, celebrate, amplify, the rewards of others, there's joy in that."

With only a handful of powerful women executives in the NBA franchises and even fewer who are Black, Williams eventually learned how to create and sustain her own happiness, create community and turn her focus outward while facing immense pressures and challenges in high-powered roles.

"And another thing to put out there is being an advocate for one another," Williams said. "So I wish someone would have sat me down in my twenties and really lined it up. And perhaps they did, and I was just 20-something, and I didn't hear them or understand them."

Williams benefitted from that kind of advocacy from a very early stage in her career. She said that she has yet to apply for a job since she left college and started her first internship. She credits women for advocating for her and paving the way for her to be considered for positions that she ultimately walked into without seeking out the opportunities herself. With every step in the journey, she continued to build her community of women and women of color in the sports industry. She remarked that, surprisingly, that advocacy hasn't been rare for her, but it certainly has been meaningful.

As the COO of the College Football Playoff, she had a role that women in the Fortune 500 rarely obtain – one with profit and loss (P&L) responsibility. Historically, those roles position leaders better to take the top spot in an organization as CEO. She took on five internships before ever claiming her first full-time position in sports, but as a former student-athlete, she was surrounded by people who could help her on her journey. She realized early, however, that those people wouldn't simply do things because she was there. She had to ask.

Being vocal about what she wanted paid off tremendously. Supportive advocates and effective, reliable sponsors also added to her positive experiences and general happiness along her climb.

The burden of resilience can stunt our healing and therefore halt sustainable happiness

We have to recognize our resilience for what it is: a result of trauma that needs to be addressed and mended before we move on.

"Due to the intersecting identities of being a woman and being Black, Black women are at risk for dual oppression and double discrimination. And, despite experiencing sexism and racism, have persevered," wrote licensed psychologist, Summer Rose, in an opinion piece in *Newsweek*.

My Black women leader clients display this exact disposition consistently, no matter who they are and where they are from. They face adversity, and they simply push through. There is no time to ruminate for too long on what happened and why. They often do not allow themselves the space to emote for too long about it. Most of us were taught growing up to simply dust ourselves off and keep it moving.

That perseverance has granted us the gift of resilience, but it comes with a cost. In fact, the resilience itself had a high price tag, and that is trauma. I call this the burden of resilience, and until recently, it has not been the norm for Black women to address it by seeking the help of a professional, whether a therapist or a personal coach. So, we carry the wounds with us to the next opportunity, although they are scabbed over. But have we actually healed?

In session after session, I raise this question: "How were you hurt in your last position?" There is always a story riddled with toxicity, racism and sexism, and either she was pushed out or narrowly escaped to a new role. She always emerges from it eventually, but she soldiers through her first 90 days and into the next opportunity. Consistently, however, I learn that they haven't taken the steps to heal from the past trauma. Their healing, for them, was the escape and the relief they feel from breaking free. Perhaps this is how our ancestors operated.

I know for certain that my mother learned to bury the pain of hurt, physical and otherwise, and keep moving forward wearing that as a crown. It's steeped in cultural norms from slavery to our faith, where suffering is centered as an honor as a follower of Christ who did the same for us.

Once, after wrapping up work and placing a routine evening commute call to my parents, no one answered the phone. I tried calling their cell phones, and neither of them answered. This was rare, so I called my sister, who hadn't heard from them either. It was clear they weren't home, so I became concerned. Eventually, after buzzing my father for about the fourth time, he answered. I would learn that they were sitting in the emergency room waiting to see a doctor.

When I asked my father why, he did his usual gatekeeping."

"Hey, Chelle. Oh yes, we're here at the emergency room because your mother had a little accident in the kitchen, but she is fine," he said.

I've learned over time that his calmness is nearly always a cause for alarm.

"What happened?" I yelled. "Is she ok?"

I would learn that she was preparing a fruit tray for her Bible Study Fellowship gathering and sliced off the tip of her finger. This horrified me.

"Where is she? Can you pass the phone?"

He did, and she was incredibly calm and peaceful as she recalled how it happened. She didn't cry out in pain or anything. She wrapped the tip of her finger in something, placed it in her purse, and calmly went upstairs to tell my father that they should probably go to the hospital.

"Had I not been bleeding so much, I probably wouldn't have called your father down when I did," she said.

I gasped.

"Are you kidding me?" I said.

The doctors had to sew the tip of her finger back on that night, and both my parents were acting as if she had endured a bee sting or something less. It's just an example of their approach to pain. And yes, she was back in the kitchen the next day chopping up something else. The experience didn't phase her one bit.

Needless to say, this severing of her finger is only symbolic of how both my parents approached trauma. There have been times when I realized that they lived through Jim Crow and the Civil Rights movement. When I asked them about their experiences, their calmness about run-ins with racists was disturbingly low-key and tranquil. Like the time my father says his father, my grandfather, was stopped on the highway in East Texas in the 1960s by a police officer for no reason. He was told to step out of the car and repeatedly berated and called 'boy' and the N-word. Daddy was a teenager when he witnessed it. His father told him to remain in the car and stay quiet while this was going on.

I asked my dad what his father said to him after that happened, and he shared that they were silent all the way to their destination and never spoke of it again. Their escape was their healing.

Our burden of resilience

Not only do vivid, horrific experiences like my father's and grandfather's cause us to approach trauma in a way that doesn't allow us to process it appropriately or heal completely, but we also learn in these moments, and they make us stronger. I learned from industrial psychology scholar Karrie Sullivan, of Culminate Strategy Group, that her company's study of the growth and fixed mindsets of top leaders and the impact of their organization's success revealed that adversity can produce people with growth mindsets, especially if we allow ourselves to learn from that adversity.

"So people who have gone through adverse situations in their careers or in their lives have had opportunities to lean into that adversity and let it change them and change the way that they think," Sullivan said. "They become more resilient, and they become better problem solvers."

This resilience in people of color is celebrated in our culture. It's why one of the first compliments we hear about Black women is that we are strong, even before we hear compliments about our intelligence. But let's ponder this for a moment. Sullivan was clear in saying that resilience is born from adversity. That's trauma. That isn't a reason to celebrate. Yes, it makes us stronger, but how exactly did we gain this strength, new perspective and problem-solving ability? It wasn't positive.

I've started calling this *the burden of resilience*. It explains a lot about my parents and others that I looked up to in their generation and older. They are some of the most incredible leaders, but they aren't so accomplished at acknowledging, processing or healing from the trauma that brought them to this point. Sullivan says this is why women and people of color who have allowed their adversity to change them and facilitate learning are some of the most incredible transformational leaders and have earned growth mindsets. She shared that this phenomenon is linked to the reasons why so many women of color are called upon to rescue companies that are on the brink of collapse or in crisis.

Seeking out superiors with growth mindsets can help increase your sense of satisfaction at work.

When we are entering new roles, we must look for indications of fixed mindsets in leadership and avoid them.

When I interviewed Karrie Sullivan on my show, The Culture Soup Podcast®, I was intrigued with how machine learning was how her company was able to examine language across company chatter, internally and externally, within minutes to determine the personalities and workstyles of those in the highest ranks in companies. She and her team could do this without even darkening the doors of those companies or meeting one employee. She shared another fact with me that could impact the happiness of underrepresented leaders like women and other people of color.

"We have a rule," she said, referring to organizations going through substantial transformation. "Growth mindset can report to growth mindset. Fixed mindset can report to growth mindset. Growth mindset can *not* report to fixed mindset."

While she emphasized that fixed mindset leaders indeed have value because they are excellent at adhering to process and ensuring things get done, they struggle with out-of-the-box thinking. In fact, when they have reports that solve problems differently than they are familiar with, there is a strong chance that they will see their growth mindset reports as a problem, and the friction will be evident in their performance evaluations and, in the worst cases, these talented leaders who can run to the risk and thrive can be pushed down or out of organizations where they more than likely could have had an incredible impact.

I recall when the big company was in the midst of a major acquisition and our organization was undergoing massive change, org charts were flying everywhere. Reflecting back, Sullivan's research shed light on my experience in a whole new way. I remember being asked by an HR leader who was leading an investigation into why I didn't receive an incentive bonus that year (and later why my role was taken from me and my team disbanded) if I believed that what was happening to me was racist in nature. Now, first of all, I wasn't the one who called HR, someone else did. To this day, that person has not made themselves known to me. However, I really appreciate the way that person tried to come to my defense. I replied to the investigator that I had no clue if what they were doing was driven by racial bias, and that was the truth. I didn't know these people. I passed them in the hall and said hello, but that was the extent of our dealings before they were put in charge of me. What I did understand was that they didn't understand what I was doing in my role, and no matter who tried to explain it to them, they were still honestly confused and didn't get it. Because they didn't understand it, I was vilified. Despite the awards and the multiple "exceeds ratings" that I'd received before they were my bosses, the scuttle that would always get back to me smacked of, "But what does she do?" And whoever shared what was being said would tell me that they were earnestly asking and truly didn't get it.

And I believed it. Even the Black man who replaced my incredible boss simply didn't understand the work I was doing with my team and couldn't explain it to his bosses. His role was to be some sort of translator, I suppose, because he was Black like me. The bonus, I'd imagine, was that perhaps they thought that I couldn't call him racist, simply because he was also Black. It was a mess.

Back then, I couldn't put into words what Sullivan described to me on the podcast so succinctly: I was reporting to fixed mindsets. They were clock punchers, micromanagers, process-over-people people, and they wanted everyone to be like them. Results to them came from media placements – coverage only. They were into tactics, and they didn't want my high-level strategy methods. As Sullivan said, we spoke totally different languages. Often, this results in the fixed mindsets getting angry about it, and their only answer to their challenge with me was to place me on a surplus list, because my work, track record, and reputation at the company were unimpeachable.

I remember telling the investigator that if I suspected any bias, perhaps it was gender-related. I had reported to all men before, but they operated differently. In fact, my leaders before this group were all white men – at least, I thought so. My immediate boss would later reveal that he was Native American, white-passing, which explained so much about him. He was one of my fiercest defenders. This new group of men would lay him off as well. But there was something else that Sullivan told me that connected the dots for me about why I felt that sexism could have been at the bottom of things, but there was no real way to prove it outside of anecdotal hearsay.

Sullivan told me that opportunistic-style fixed mindsets are great for sales organizations but if you accumulate too much of that in one place in an organization, the result is what she called "bro culture" that is ultimately detrimental to the success of the company. And this crew indeed had the ultimate "bro" culture.

"You end up with more competition," she said. "The conversation goes from 'How do we change business?' and 'How do we really become a game changer for our clients?' into, 'How about those Rams?' And it's a very different kind of discussion around the water cooler. And as that company or that discussion starts to shift one way or the other, so does the performance of the company."

Shutting down social and traditional media can do wonders for our happiness.

We must recognize the media as the distraction it can be and the disruptor to our peace that it has proven to be.

I remember the day that we learned that Breonna Taylor's killers would not be charged for her murder. This was about a year before her family would win millions in the settlement of a wrongful death lawsuit. My thoughts went immediately to my community of leaders. While we were still largely working from home, most of them had better access to television news content than they would if they were working from the office. I also saw my social media feed light up with the news. That's when it occurred to me that Black women leaders were in crisis and likely had no outlet to process their feelings while in the midst of their work hours. I promptly arranged a free emergency group coaching session to gather these women so that they could.

It was clear that the news impacted these women deeply. Whether they had heard the news in the moment or later, the impact would no doubt be the same, but exposure during work hours left them with very little space to emote in the way they would have liked to. I was happy to provide a safe space for them to open up and share. But then it occurred to me that the way we receive information is now more pervasive than ever.

When the news of Tyre Nichols' killing at the hands of Memphis police officers broke, it was hard to avoid. It seemed to be in surround sound, and news like this has an impact on Black women leaders as it does most Black people who hear about it. However, the news of the planned release of the video was doubly traumatic. It was announced like a movie premiere, which was a little grotesque, but it was a good heads-up for Black people who wanted to avoid viewing the video on television or social media platforms. However, just knowing that there was more terrifying footage available for consumption was enough to rattle most Black Americans.

Shielding oneself from the media can be an extraordinary act of self-care and psychological safety for high-performing Black women leaders and, for that matter, anyone. However, for Black people, it is an extremely heroic act of self-preservation because it is hard to watch or scroll without seeing the exploitation of our culture or our bodies in one way or the other. I can't tell you how the simple act of turning off my television and muting my social media alerts has preserved my peace and kept me smiling during some of the most challenging times in our nation. Going dark on traditional and social media removes that one last layer of confusion so that I can return to a calm mind. Neuroscience shows us that if we can achieve a calm mind, we can regain our focus, which is required for insight. Insight is crucial to creativity, innovation, and, ultimately, productivity. In short, protecting your peace keeps you in the game, and this is very important to Black women because what we see in the media about our community, apparently impacts us more than any other group.

The State of Consumer Engagement 2021 © Horowitz Research study confirms that media, both social and traditional, impacts Black women in such a way that they have stronger feelings about it compared to Black men. Compared to 47% of Black men, 55% of Black women said they strongly agree that seeing so much video everywhere of violence against Black Americans is having a negative impact on their mental health. That same study reveals that Black women tend to carry more of the emotional impact of what they see in the media, with 59% of them agreeing that they are fearful for their families and their own safety in today's socio-political environment. That's compared to 55% of Black men. That gap widens when you compare Black women and white women fearing for their own families. Only 44% of white women strongly agreed with the statement. We saw Black women, and women in general, become quite vocal about the impact of media on their mental health long before the pandemic and George Floyd's murder, which was captured with cell phone footage. By the time we witnessed Philando Castille's shooting live streamed on Facebook, Black women were among the most vocal as they started memes on social media proclaiming that they would be "calling in Black" to work so that they could stay home for a mental health break. That was 2016. During the 2020 lockdown, although videos like Castille's played out on the news or on newsfeeds with the same impact, white-collar Black women found solace in the fact that they were safely behind computer screens while working from home.

"Calling in Black" was first coined by a professional Black woman/creator, Evelyn From The Internets, in a YouTube video that went viral. In the video, she introduced the term and then walked viewers through what it meant and how to do it. She was all of us, wanting to bury herself in her covers and turn over in bed after a phone call to the office unapologetically saying she was taking a mental health day, but in far more colorful terms.

The term caught on with Middle Easterners and Indians posting on social media about calling in Brown, and even some organizations hosted town hall meetings urging Black employees to share their experiences of wanting to call in Black.

Taking a break from the media doesn't solve the problem of violence against Black people, but it most certainly provides some temporary psychological safety so that Black women and other people of color can find a brief respite in order to focus and stay positive. Every little bit counts.

Coaching Questions

What one small step can you take today to reclaim your happiness on your leadership journey to the C-Suite?

_____
_____
_____
_____
_____
_____
_____
_____
_____
_____
_____
_____
_____
_____
_____
_____
_____
_____
_____
_____
_____
_____
_____

What anecdote in this chapter inspired an action in you? What action will you take, and what barriers do you need to navigate?

What resources or support might you need to begin to secure your happiness on your leadership journey?

If you had more happiness in this very moment, what would you do that you aren't already doing right now?

How can you encourage or applaud another woman in a way that may inspire happiness in their journey?

7 AFFIRMATION #6

"I AM A VALUABLE LEADER, AND I WILL BE OPEN TO OTHER ORGANIZATIONS THAT WILL DEMONSTRATE THAT TO ME."

Secret: The fastest way to increase your salary and get promoted is to leave.

The question is always a dreaded one for me, but it is never the first. The first question that inevitably leads to the one that makes me cringe is, "Where are you from?" When I tell them Dallas, there's usually some shock. "Really? I would have thought Chicago or D.C.," they always say. And while this used to offend me because why couldn't I be from Texas, and why did I have to be from somewhere else if the statement was intended as some sort of a compliment? Now that I'm older, I can get past that one, but the question that follows typically gives me angst. Until now, I've never admitted to it aloud.

"So, have you lived in Dallas all your life?"

Shoot.

But then I answer, giving the obligatory exception because living here all my life seems less progressive or up-and-coming.

"Well, for a sliver of a second, I did live part-time in Atlanta. If you blinked, you would have missed it. I commuted between the two cities, with an address here in Dallas and one there. I considered doing this in Chicago since I was always up there and had a satellite office there."

Deep down, I knew that question didn't require all that explanation. What was bothering me inside? I knew that there were times in my life when I wanted to leave Dallas. Choosing my college was likely the first time. As quiet as it was kept, I would have loved to have explored Fisk, Hampton University or another HBCU. The second time was when I received an offer from a Houston television station to produce the morning and noon news shows.

My parents had quite a hold on me as a young adult, primarily through guilt and fear of disappointing them. I'm not alone. This can be a result of cultural norms, whether racial, regional or religious. If you were brave enough to leave, you would no doubt face their wrath in the form of sheer silence or the extreme opposite. Either way, you were choosing a life of misery.

Honor your father and mother is one of the most abused scriptures in some cultures. It has little to do with career choices as an adult when it is time to leave the nest, and yet, I've seen this happen to Black and Brown adult children who are guilted into staying close to their parents because they say it's best. Ultimately, it benefits them more than it benefits you, but at 18 or even in your mid-twenties, it's really hard to see. I also believe that because I took the unbeaten path in my family and declined a teaching career in favor of the media, the decision to ultimately stay in one market was career-limiting. In TV news, to move up, you have to move out, but because I didn't have the desire to be on camera at the time, it was easier to climb in a single market.

I've had my share of regretful reflections as I progressed in my career, which was by no means an intentionally plotted one. As I met and supported clients at major brands, and had C-Suite leaders go on about my work and call me smart, many of them with Ivy League degrees, I wondered how much better I would have been if I had gone to Harvard or Howard. I was no doubt a motivated, go-getter, but it wasn't directed at any one goal except doing great at what was in front of me at that moment.

Television wasn't the only career where more upward mobility was achievable if you simply packed your bag and moved, and I knew it. In fact, your choice of marriage partners also expands. So if you choose to stay in one market or at any one company, you are choosing to limit your entire life's potential.

Why are we trying so hard to live our lives the way the previous generation did? In this volatile market that is all change and very little time to ponder it, perhaps we should stay on our toes, prepared to pivot to the next company, even if it is in a completely different part of the country or world.

Identify the real reason why you're staying.

It's interesting. My women leaders know exactly why they need to leave, but are pretty murky about why they should stay. It typically comes down to it being the path of least resistance, primarily from themselves. My Sister, if you stay in one place, your ascent will be slower. It will take years, and it isn't guaranteed, as companies are moving towards more agile workforces and outsourcing capabilities increasingly. I knew my why, and it was painful to admit to myself, but even I understood that while my opportunity was limited by one market for some unfortunate reasons, I never thought my future was tied to any single company. This mindset not only kept me sane, it kept me engaged, energized and entrepreneurial.

Staying seems safer. But who does it really benefit?

Many leaders believe that staying in one place is safe, and it probably benefits your organization more than it does you. You can count on the predictability of your pay, that it won't increase quickly in most cases, that you will work on the same widgets, even in different business units, until you retire (if you manage to dodge downsizing), and that your 401k will stay comfortably tucked away and growing at a steady pace. Some of us put that brand of safety over psychological safety and will stay and stew in a toxic environment that we know is hurting us emotionally and physically, simply to say that we stayed. That's somewhat like a bad marriage that no one knows is bad because you're hosting your 25th-anniversary party, and everyone's invited.

I've had clients explore the idea of leaving their current position and posit that they may find yet another toxic boss, or they ask, "What if it doesn't work out? What if I don't like it there?" And so they stay. I ask them instead, "What if it *does* work out?" "What if your next boss isn't toxic?" and "What do you lose out on if you stay?" "What could you do now to limit the chances that it doesn't work out or you get another toxic boss?" And "What if it doesn't work out or you get another toxic boss? What can you do then?" The answer is typically, find another position.

Career experts agree that the fastest way to increase your title and compensation is to leave. Each of the women leaders whom I interviewed for this book did not remain in one place, they moved to the next opportunity that supported them and their goals. The pandemic accelerated their movement. The so-called "Great Resignation" happened. I chose to call it the "Great Opt Out" because women discovered they had more choices and they had value. The 2022 Women in the Workplace Study by McKinsey and LeanIn.org called it the "Great Breakup," reporting that women leaders were switching jobs at the highest rates ever seen, and at higher rates than men in leadership. The report said for every woman director who was promoted, two left the company. This is not good news for organizations, but it places the woman leader at an advantage because organizations are having difficulty holding on to top female talent, and it's even more of an issue holding on to the most talented women of color. For the woman leader, this means more opportunity and more choices.

The highest-ranking women leaders did not stay

Now, more than ever, the time is right to get up and move, whether it is across town or across the country. Staying stagnant in one company is ill-advised. I mentioned earlier that Dr. Kecia Kelly had moved many times, but what would you say if I told you that it was 10 times to 10 cities? One of them twice. But that's okay because it was in Hawaii. That is probably more moving than most, and with Dr. Kelly's military background as a former commissioned officer in the Army and as a child of a military family, she is uniquely built for that challenge. Perusing the Linkedin profiles of the two Black women CEOs in the Fortune 500, I discovered how true it is that moving means more success. Thasunda Brown Duckett spent several years at Chase and its family of brands before landing at the top at TIAA, and before that, Fannie Mae. Rosalind Brewer, CEO at Walgreens Boots, had several stops before she landed there, including Walmart/Sam's Club, Starbucks, and Kimberly-Clark. Both women only list their last few positions on Linkedin, as most smart executives do. In both cases, these women spent no more than 5 years in each position, and on average 3-4 years, before they moved up to their next E- or C-Suite position. In fact, Brewer accelerated into several C- level roles after leaving Kimberly-Clark, where she made it to VP after 22 years there.

What GenXers can learn from the Millennials

The fact is, C-Suite ascension happens fairly quickly for those willing to go to the opportunity instead of waiting for it to come to them. Take Emily K. Graham, Chief Equity and Impact Officer, Omnicom, one of the youngest C-Suite leaders in the global agency world. She rose to her position at the strategic communications conglomerate after a brief stint as Chief Diversity Officer (CDO) at Fleishman Hillard (FH) and only four years as Partner there, 8 months as Senior Partner, and another eight months as CDO. Before her time at FH, she spent less than 5-6 years respectively at two other global agencies. Graham is a millennial and definitely has the millennial mindset that GenXers should adopt. Career and leadership experts all agree that leaders should not be in one position for more than 3-5 years before seeking their next. She isn't the only one.

I mentioned in *No Thanks: 7 Ways to Say I'll Just Include Myself* that Bozoma Saint John modeled the behavior of knowing her value and then moving in that power to the next opportunity. Graham mentioned her again in our conversation because she publically chided a publication that essentially called Saint John's moves job hopping.

"I took offense when I saw her go to Netflix and there was an article written in the advertising industry about her being a jumper," she said. "I remember what they said. I was unhappy. Then I wrote them, and I said, 'The audacity of you to call this talented, upwardly mobile black woman, anything less than hugely successful and talented.' She has no obligation to stay anywhere that's not serving her.'"

Graham went on to comment that high-performing, excellent Black women have "the audacity to believe in us."

"And when we feel like that value is not showing itself, we're not waiting for the affirmation. We're saying, you know what? This doesn't work," she said. "And we start to be more selective of opportunities. But also, we start to be more authentic in what you expect and require early on. So that we are going into spaces where we can be who we are and not code-switch. You're able to be in the C-suite."

She went on, "And that's one thing I'm grateful for, because I can be who I am, read all the articles, listen to all the interviews because what I wrote, what I say is exactly the way I'm going to lead once I get into the seat in this boardroom. And that's what I think is the key to that freedom—and freedom and confidence looks good on you. And it allows you to unlock potential and not worry so much."

Higher pay and better compensation aren't the only reasons to leave

That Women in the Workplace study shared that there was even more in it for women leaders to leave their companies. Besides facing microaggressions on a daily basis and frequent pushback on promotions, the data shows that women leaders are seeking a different culture of work.

> *"Women leaders are significantly more likely than men leaders to leave their jobs because they want more flexibility or because they want to work for a company that is more committed to employee well-being and DEI. And over the last two years, these factors have only become more important to women leaders: they are more than 1.5 times as likely as men at their level to have left a previous job because they wanted to work for a company that was more committed to DEI."*

So there is a good chance that you can find a better, less toxic, environment than if you stay, thanks to more awareness by companies who spend time pouring over research like Women in the Workplace. But a word to the wise: no one organization is perfect in this area, but leaders can count on the honeymoon phase and a good run at most positions before they go South; and Sis, that's between 18 months and three to five years. That tracks with how long companies plan to keep workers these days anyway, so you might as well continue your job hunt, networking, relationships with recruiters, and plan your exit before your engagement at the organization has the chance to turn. Leave on a high note. It's surprising to clients when I ask them a week into a new position what they are planning to do next, but this is the reason why.

Coaching Questions

What are you giving up on if you stay more than 3-5 years?

What is your exit strategy?

What is your biggest concern about leaving your current position?

How can you plan to navigate that challenge?

What next step would I take in the next year in my leadership journey if I weren't afraid?

Identify a high-performing Millennial woman leader. What have you noticed about how they approach their career, and what can you learn from them?

8 AFFIRMATION #7

"I AM ENTITLED TO THE ADVOCACY AND MENTORSHIP OF AT LEAST TWO HIGH-POWERED WHITE MEN."

Secret: Many Black women executive leaders point to white men in their careers as being the most helpful in their leadership quest.

The year was 2005, and I met a blonde-haired, blue-eyed man who had worked his way up to CEO from rolling burritos at the same fast food chain, and I was fortunate enough to tell his story again and again because my boutique PR shop was their agency of record. Despite his significant role in turning the super regional brand around, he was quite humble, and he began to call me his "wing woman."

This man was also a fierce supporter of The Executive Leadership Council (ELC) At the time, I knew very little about it, only that the founder of one of the hair care brands we represented was one of the founding members of ELC. Supporting this CEO and his quick-service brand wasn't incredibly lucrative, but it was indeed a pleasure. My team and I made so many solid connections in the industry, whether it be media or franchise, even other quick-service brands. In fact, it was because of the excellent work that we did, that this executive introduced me to more CEOs and even franchisees. It is safe to say that this executive was key to growing our restaurant and retail portfolio of clients because he simply believed in our work. But it didn't stop there. Long after I'd closed my agency and began working for another global agency as a senior vice president, this executive not only remained in touch, but he made a few attempts to hire me. While I was working at the big company, he made his desire known. He wouldn't be the only white man who saw the value of my work and not only advocated and sponsored me, but at some point, he even worked as an accomplice, asking his chief brand officer to write a letter of recommendation for me, to accompany his own, for an officer role for another organization since they held a multi-year sponsorship deal with them. That chief brand officer didn't know me, but he simply went on the word of his boss and the work that my agency had done for the brand, which had become a part of their company's history.

This chief brand officer was a believer. So much so that after I left the big company, he tried to hire me—twice.

This is the kind of rabid fandom that is needed to move career needles and move great leaders into their rightful roles in the E- and C-Suites. In fact, I had a few white men who went to bat for me in more ways than one. When I received that call from the big company where I was told that they would stop the search if I put myself forward, not only was that offer put forth by a white man who was my very first boss in public relations, the actual hiring manager, the SVP of corporate communications, was the one who empowered him to make that statement. This would later be the officer whose office I visited a couple of times before I left the big company. He was the one who was not only encouraging me to stay but opening the doors so that I could. He was also the one who gave me the mandate when I came to him with the concept that would evolve into a ground-breaking inclusion marketing strategy that would change the way the marketing organizations worked together in their efforts to reach untapped markets and mitigate reputational risks before they happened.

Allow me to say that none of these men were necessarily liberal in their political leanings. They ran the gamut, from Republican to a self-described "progressive" to a Libertarian. None of them allowed their political leanings to drive what was best for the business, and in their eyes, I was not only good for the business, but had rockstar qualities, and they had no hesitation in putting my name forward again and again.

This experience is not unique to my story. In fact, every high-powered Black woman that I've interviewed for this book and previous ones had similar stories to tell. Andrea Williams, chief experience officer at the Utah Jazz, shared her experience.

"I had an amazing boss, or commissioner, there who's now retired, Jim Delaney, who is probably the smartest, most successful collegiate sports administrator that's ever been," she said. "And he was a great leader. And he took very good care of me when there were opportunities for advancement, when there were opportunities for exposure, when there was opportunity for growth, he provided that. And he was a white male. But he was there. He was supportive."

Earlier in this book I raised a question: Could it be that Black women are looking for sponsors in all the wrong places? I believe we are. Conventional wisdom says, "If you see it, you can be it." So we look for those who look like us. However, when you ask the Black women who have actually made it to the C-Suite, they tell a totally different story.

The truth is in the numbers

I was curious, so I surveyed 100 high-performing Black women to tell me, based on race and gender, who had been the most helpful and the most hindrance to their leadership journey. Overwhelmingly, these Black women leaders pointed to white men and other Black women as being the most helpful. While white men and other Black women tied for being the most supportive in the corporate workspace (41% each), nearly 60% of respondents pointed to white women as being the biggest hindrance. That was followed by 44% saying white men as the second most problematic to Black women thriving in the corporate workspace. Another 22% pointed at other women of color as not acting as allies, followed by Black men at 9%.

In fact, so many Black women have been told that white men are the enemy, full stop. So many of us have had poor experiences with white men, but in my research, in my experiences, in many conversations, and even a survey or two, Black women overwhelmingly point to a segment of white men who have actually made something significant happen for them in their careers. But before you shower them with praise of benevolence, when you peel back the onion, it may be a combination of factors that add up to this reality. Consider this:

It's a game of numbers.

There are far more white men in big business, and far more of them are successful and in a position to actually take unquestioned, swift action. Dr. Christopher C. Butts, a diversity, equity, inclusion, learning and development expert, shared that because there are so many powerful white male senior executives, Black women leaders have shared that they've had white male sponsors and it worked out well.

"When you think about the number of black women in the C-suite, I think it's 3-4% total…with the most recent data." Butts said.

"And if that's the total amount in the C-suite, you need your advocates, you need your sponsors, you need your allies. And yes, if you find the right white male ally, who is truly an ally and a sponsor, and wants to advocate on your behalf, it's very, very helpful."

Master coach LaFern Kitt Batie said that her clients say they have more supportive white men taking action in their careers, and it is an experience that she can also relate to. "Many times they will say, and it was my personal experience too, that this white man helped me, gave me more information, gave me more insight," Batie said.

In contrast, there are very few Black women in these top positions. Therefore, if you have Black women leaders in extremely powerful spaces, you may not have access to her, or she may have what Batie calls "the only syndrome." Some refer to this as the Queen Bee syndrome, and that mindset considers sponsoring another Black woman high risk.

"It's the mindset of, I don't want to jeopardize my role because I know how hard it is to get here," Batie said.

Dr. Butts believes that while it is important to seek out sponsors that look like you, the reality is that because there are so few Black leaders at the top level of the Fortune 500, Black women should indeed be open to sponsors and mentors that do not look like them because once you get to the C-Suite, your differences become more pronounced and the microaggressions increase. He said that it's a reality of the structure of corporate America. After all, the word 'corporate' means 'one body,' and Black women simply don't fit the mold as easily because of their color and gender.

"The system works that way, because it says, Hey, you're different. You're not like everyone else here," Butts said. "And they voiced that to you. Those microaggressions come constantly, and they voiced that to you. So then you are thinking, oh my gosh, I have this heightened demand on me from this now C-suite group that I'm with, and I want to help others, but I'm so frightened to do so, because what if they don't perform? Or what if they're not what I know they can be because of all the added pressures that unduly come upon them as they continue their growth? It's, unfortunately, the way the system has been designed and set up, but it's been designed and set up on purpose that way."

It's the reality of privilege.

Membership has its privileges, and this isn't about credit cards. It's about who is centered in corporate America. If your actions will likely not be questioned or interrogated as much as someone of color, there are certain things you can get done a bit faster than anyone else without risking your brand equity or reputation. Batie said that her clients report that their white male bosses are willing to take more risks.

"So my white male counterpart might be able to take a chance and the risk of championing or sponsoring someone, not turning out exactly as that person desired, but it's not a mark on that person's career," Batie said.

It's a privilege Black women do not wield, even when they make it to the C-Suite. Emily K. Graham recalls what it felt like the first several times she was "at the table," and she said that if there is a piece of advice she could give other Black women, something she wished she knew then that she knows now, it's that a position in the C-Suite as a Black woman, and in her case, a young Black woman, isn't all rainbows and unicorns.

"It's going to be achy and odd walking into your power the first few times," she said. "Wondering how people are going to react to you. If they're going to treat you equitably, and if you will command the respect; if you will cower [at] the microaggression…because you're not really sure until you get into the scenario."

Graham continued, "You want to be thoughtful, but we are Black women, and we're constantly struggling with, if we react wrong or right. That's a blemish that would be lasting."

These are issues that white men don't deal with as much, so it follows that they have the emotional and leadership equity and real estate to offer a leader they want to sponsor more immediately. Black women do not have this luxury. We understand that one misstep can be viewed as a blemish on our career and ultimately mean our legacy as a leader.

The threat isn't as great.

White men innately understand their dominance in our culture. They pop out of the womb believing and knowing they are in charge. They also understand the social caste, that Black women, because of their race and gender, pose little if any threat to their stature. In fact, in the patriarchy that is core to white supremacy, women have their place, and she could never threaten his trajectory.

"They don't see me as competition, and in their mind, I'm not attaining where they are," said Graham. "So it's going to make them feel much better to be my mentor and my sponsor to make paths for me because in their mind, well, I'm not competing with them."

"I think part of it is they tend to look at when they see a high performer, they tend to look at that as a win for them, " Batie said. " This is someone who I can support, but who also makes me shine. He goes in and they are all about whatever helps make them or the team shine. They don't see that as a competition. They see that as competitive positioning." White men operate without the threat that perhaps another Black woman or any other woman might perceive."

White men can wield their privilege on behalf of someone who is an actual rainmaker, acknowledge that skill and talent, and still stand tall. Not so for other women or women of color advocating for Black women, and unfortunately, not the case for other Black men who might seem to have a leg up simply because they are male. While they may make it to the sports bar or golf tee with their white male colleagues, Black men have to navigate what the threat of another man can manifest – so they spend much of their time attempting to temper that trope daily.

So this privilege makes advocacy for others who do not look like them so absolutely effortless for white men, at least when you compare it to the advocacy and sponsorship that Black women wield on behalf of others.

Dr. Kecia M. Kelly recalls taking a Chief Nursing Officer role and immediately began working for pay equity for her diverse teams. It was important to her, and she recalled it as an effort that took some "jumping through hoops." She had put their interests before her own. But if you recall that $50,000 bump in pay that she received because she didn't negotiate her salary on the way into the position? It was a white man, her boss, who simply walked up to her one day, and nonchalantly told her that he made it happen.

"On that Monday, my administrator, he just hands me this piece of paper, and he just says, 'I've gotten you a payroll adjustment to get you within market with the other CNOs within [the company].' I looked at it, and it was $50,000." And he did it all, seemingly, without breaking a sweat.

The number of progressive white men has increased over the years.

Let's face it. Some white men are just tired of the rap they get, so there is some good that can come from being on the right side of history – a better brand, a better reputation. Still, some honestly believe in fairness and justice and want to judge people by their talent and abilities.

"If they can leave in their legacy, the fact that they advanced and helped a young Black person, well, that makes people feel good," Graham said.

Dr. Christopher Butts ponders whether there is a segment of the white male leadership that is more enlightened. He himself is a white man.

"I would like to, and maybe naively I would like to say that there is a newer generation of those white male C-suite executives. And with that newer generation of them, there is that increased awareness: Butts said. "There is the awareness that as a white male C-suite executive, I haven't benefited from white privilege. And I'm hoping that at some point, they deem and determine I have benefited from this and now I need to see what I can do to help others, or how can I be of benefit or a service to others? That's what I would like or hope to believe, but I'm not really sure."

Whatever the reasons white men have been the most helpful to Black women leaders (because they also appear on the list of people who have hindered their leadership aspirations, second only to white women according to the majority of those surveyed), it is easy to surmise that Black women are finding it difficult to know who they can trust and may not be eager to engage with people who do not look like them in order to push their leadership aspirations forward. Trust erosion leads to disillusionment, but if Black women leaders are willing to push through the fear and open themselves up to the possibility that some of these relationships could work in their favor, the chances of their progression up the corporate ladder increase.

COACHING QUESTIONS

What can you do to create the kind of visibility that will attract a white male sponsor who can make a difference in your leadership aspirations?

If you have white male advocates, what can be done to move them from passive advocacy to full sponsorship?

How might you be able to decipher the white male leaders who could be solid mentors and advocates for you?

Who do you already know that is working in your favor, and how might ignite more action from your white male mentor or sponsor?

_____
_____
_____
_____
_____
_____
_____
_____
_____
_____
_____
_____
_____
_____
_____
_____
_____
_____
_____
_____
_____
_____
_____
_____
_____

What can you do to open your tribe up to more people who do not look like or work like you do?

9 ONE MORE THING...

A LETTER TO MY BROTHERS

Dear, Black men...

There is a special place in my heart for you because so many of you had an impact on my life, beginning with my father. I've had so many positive models of strength, leadership and character in men like you. I could point to my brother-in-law, cousins, uncles and even pastors who have impacted me personally, so I know what you can be: champions, sanctuaries, confidants, inspirations, intellects, leaders, sounding boards, mentors, friends, brothers. You have been granted a unique opportunity to be all of these things to your sisters. Because our culture has a keen and nearly perfected sense of community, you can be so much to even those you do not have close relationships with, specifically as colleagues, but then also as potential dating relationships and partners.

That survey I conducted with 100 Black women leaders revealed something that concerned me. When asked by gender and by race, which group had been the most helpful in their careers, you ranked third, with white men coming in first, tied with Black women.

I'd love to see you move up higher on that list.

I've been so encouraged, however, by the husbands that I've come into contact with through my women leader clients, and equally so by the men leaders that I coach who are also husbands and fathers.

This is where I had my breakthrough. These men that I've encountered through my practice have some shared traits and perhaps they set the standard for men who support women leaders aspiring for top positions in business.

They are open to female leadership. The fact that men have contracted me to guide them through their leadership journey reveals that they are not only okay with the idea that a woman can support them in areas of business and leadership, they all admit that my services make them better men at home with their wives and children as well as at work.

They see their wives and partners as human first as well as uniquely talented.

When men humanize women, they tend to empathize better. Men with empathy have higher emotional intelligence. They may not be perfect, but they tend to be able to identify with women as not so different from themselves. So cheering for their partners comes easier, listening to their challenges isn't a burden and she is far more relatable. They don't buy into the TikTok psychology of "masculine and feminine energy" because it has no scientific basis and the concept veers into stereotypical roles. They don't expect us to be their mothers or grandmothers. They honor our uniqueness and adaptivity in this brave new, digital world.

These men want to see their partners thrive at home and work. When things get tough at work on the way up the ladder, they see how they can support their partners at home first, spending more time or lending a hand or offering to outsource. They also seek and invest in ways to support their partners in their leadership journey. Perhaps hiring a coach or encouraging her to take continued education or seek certifications, go to that conference or leadership development program. They may pick up the slack around the house and with the kids, leaving time for her to take a weekend at the spa or simply get away alone or with girlfriends.

They value listening first and foster an inquisitive spirit. A genuine interest goes a long way for partners who have leadership aspirations, and if it is in an area that is unfamiliar, these men take the time to learn. They do not shut her down when she's talking about things that excite her that are business oriented, and they are open to listening actively and engaging without judgment or prescription.

At work and beyond, they speak up for their sisters. It makes an incredible difference when women know that they can count on you to speak up or advocate for them in rooms and spaces that are male-dominated. When a Black man does this, Black women leaders know they aren't alone, and believe me, she will return the favor when it's time.

These men generally realize that while both of you face challenges because of race, he understands or wants to learn how gender compounds things for women. Again, this takes a degree of empathy and a letting go of sorts – a letting go of the traumatized Olympic Games of "who really has it worse." He knows that his problems are unique to him, and her challenges are not only different but legitimate. There's nothing worse than a Black man who Karen's harder than Karen, or who will "All Lives Matter" you when you raise an issue that is uniquely intersectional.

He enters spaces and makes room for everyone. If what we know to be true about privilege applies to Karen as a problematic white woman who enters a space and automatically assumes she is in charge and thrusts that self-appointed authority on everyone, it follows that men, no matter what color, can and often do wield that same brand of privilege. The supportive Black man doesn't automatically condescend or go into teaching and leading mode simply because he sees you. We want colleagues at work and partners at home and in dating without an assumed reporting structure, and we aren't looking for father figures.

L. Michelle Smith

We receive enough negativity in the world as it is to experience it from partners, friends and colleagues

While it excites me when I'm on the road speaking or I receive DMs and notes from my brothers that share after a message or reading my books that they are enlightened and have a better understanding that Black women have a compounded challenge as double outsiders, it is equally as disappointing when I meet perfect strangers who neg me simply because I entered a room.

Just recently, I joined a speaking engagement on one of the many video platforms that allows you to have virtual backstage engagement. As the speakers and moderators gathered, we greeted each other. Some of us had worked together before, others had not. There was one speaker who I was excited to meet. He was an attorney who had made a name for himself. He entered backstage a little late, but everyone still greeted him kindly, including myself. As we entered the virtual room, we were to type our names as we wanted them to be seen on screen during the event. I did that. I entered my name, and since it was our alma mater, I entered the two years that I'd graduated.

So when this well-respected attorney finally entered backstage, he spoke to everyone. We were all on a first-named basis, despite there being accomplished PhDs on the platform, or so I thought. So I greeted him with his first name. He could have done the same, but instead, he said, "Hello, L. Michelle Smith, '93, '95," and he nearly snarled and snickered when he did it. There was an awkward pause on the platform, by now, there were about seven of us on screen. So I said, "Hello, Jamal." (I've changed his name here.) "I'm not sure why you read my entire super out loud, but ok."

The Ph.D. who moderated also happened to be one of the most senior and tenured professors on faculty with me at the communication college. When she introduced me, she went to great lengths to emphasize that I had two degrees from the university, and added some extra hyperbole to my bio, clearly in an effort to right the wrong that she witnessed backstage.

The tragedy in this scenario is that we were all Black, and often other Black women have learned to say something when they see something, while Black men stand by; mostly because they are oblivious to passive, verbal assaults masked as good-natured banter. However, Black men are often the assailants in these situations. This attorney wouldn't be the first.

The manager who called to tell me I was laid off was a Black man and spent the year leading up to it doing the dirty work of others based on unfounded criticism and vitriol against me. It was more disappointing to me than the white people who put him up to it.

Dating has become a complete waste of time for intellectual women who are leaders because of the so-called "alpha male" mentalities and narcissistic behaviors of men who say they are fed up with these so-called "modern women" who show interest in things outside of the home and find value in themselves.

It is even tough for women leaders to communicate with platonic male friends who espouse and spew the same rhetoric about women because he believes in role assignments for men and women. He has no problem suggesting that women endure the negging and narcissistic behavior because "sometimes all a man needs is a good woman to get him to do better." Or that friend may say things like, "You know that you would love it if you didn't have to work and all your bills were paid." And these men, like some of the most liberal and progressive white people, are champions of diversity, equity and inclusion but don't see their role in the undoing of it when they dehumanize women with statements like these.

Sexism, racism and other xenophobias are conjoined multiples. Where one exists, you can be sure that the others are lurking nearby, even if it manifests as self-hatred.

So my brothers, I believe that you can be some of the most powerful allies in our tribes both inside the home and in the workplace, but please examine, explore and deconstruct the cultural constructs that you have about women, especially Black women. It is paramount to your being that champion, sanctuary, confidant, inspiration, intellect, leader, sounding board, mentor, friend… brother.

I believe in you.

Believe in us.

Coach L. Michelle

***

10 COACHING GUIDE

32 POWERFUL QUESTIONS TO LEAD YOU TO HAPPINESS AND THE C-SUITE

***Think** about the answer to your question. **Write** your answer down in your journal along with any other thoughts you may have. Then **share** your thoughts with a mentor or coach so that you can map out a strategy. Mindfulness moments like these will ignite ah-ha moments as you soldier on to the C-Suite.*

1. How will you apply the idea of strategic likeability to move forward in your quest for senior executive leadership?

2. Which combination of positive emotions will you tap into in order to reach for happiness despite challenges in the workplace?
3. Finally, own the affirmation. Write it, and then add proof so that your mind can engage this positive thought with logic and reason: I.e., "I am likable and bring value to any space because... [Fill in the blank with a past experience that proves the affirmation.]
4. How will you shift your mindset and actions at the prospect of new sponsorship so that your career outcome doesn't depend solely on their actions or lack of action?
5. How will you open yourself up to more sponsorship that may not look like you moving forward?
6. When you have made it to executive senior leadership or the C-Suite, how will you approach sponsorship differently after reading Chapter 2?
7. What new questions will you ask when approached with a new offer or opportunity that you haven't asked in the past?
8. What is your market value, and how will you find that out?
9. What other perks can the organization offer you that you never considered before?
10. What is your vision for your life, and how do you want your next opportunity to support that vision?
11. What do you need to say to yourself to know that asking for the test title and the best compensation is something *that you deserve?*

12. How will you approach dating and marriage differently now that you are clear on the importance of a supportive partnership?
13. What are some of the issues that are sticking points for you and your partner or whomever you may be involved with?
14. If you are married, how will you begin to address issues that may be holding you back from your leadership aspirations?
15. What old ways of thinking might you need to let go of at home as a woman leader?
16. What behavior shifts might you make that will improve your dating, relationship or marriage, keeping your leadership aspirations in mind?
17. What tough conversations do you need to have with your partner that might clear the path for your aspirations and for yours together?
18. What one small step can you take today to reclaim your happiness on your leadership journey to the C-Suite?
19. What anecdote in this chapter inspired an action in you? What action will you take, and what barriers do you need to navigate?
20. What resources or support might you need to begin to secure your happiness on your leadership journey?
21. If you had more happiness in this very moment, what would you do that you aren't already doing right now?
22. How can you encourage or applaud another woman in a way that may inspire happiness in their journey?
23. What are you giving up on if you stay more than 3-5 years?

24. What is your exit strategy?
25. What is your biggest concern about leaving your current position?
26. How can you plan to navigate that challenge?
27. What next step would I take in the next year in my leadership journey if I weren't afraid?
28. What can you do to create the kind of visibility that will attract a white male sponsor who can make a difference in your leadership aspirations?
29. If you have white male advocates, what can be done to move them from passive advocacy to full sponsorship?
30. How might you be able to decipher the white male leaders who could be solid mentors and advocates for you?
31. Who do you already know that is working in your favor, and how might ignite more action from your white male mentor or sponsor?
32. What can you do to open your tribe up to more people who do not look like or work like you do?

THE 7 SECRETS CHEAT SHEET

WHAT YOU NEED TO KNOW TO GET TO HAPPY & GET TO THE C-SUITE AS A WOMAN OF COLOR

1. It isn't simply who you know, it's who likes you and the value you bring.
2. Some sponsors are all talk and no action. Have a plan.
3. Certain wealth-building opportunities only present themselves to professionals after they achieve a certain level in corporate America. The key is to reach that level, and it isn't as high as you might think.
4. Your choice of a partner will determine if you get to the C-Suite, and your journey might be a lonely one. So be prepared.

5. If you aren't happy, reaching your leadership potential will be difficult.
6. The fastest way to increase your salary and get promoted is to leave.
7. Many Black women executive leaders point to white men in their careers as being the most helpful in their leadership quest.

ACKNOWLEDGEMENTS

Can we do this like the old church again?

First, giving honor to God…my pastor, Dr. Tony Evans and his incredible family that lead the Oak Cliff Bible Fellowship Church, especially the choir, that prayed for me through a very challenging time. I had to place this book on hold for nearly a year dealing with challenges that I eventually overcame with the help of God, and I'm so thankful. The ministry of OCBF inspires me every day to continue in the spirit of ministry in my practice, especially the music ministry and the Free at Last counseling ministry led by Dr. Guy Earle, where I serve as one of the only life coach co-facilitators. This wonderful community of people reached out by email and by phone to pray for me and my family, and it meant so much and ultimately got me back on track to finish this book.

To my parents, James and Media Smith, who have been so extremely supportive of my practice, speaking and author journey. They are such great sports when it comes to my sharing stories about them, my childhood and young adulthood, the good and bad. Thank you.

To my wonderfully smart and beautiful daughter Joni, an author in denial (for now), but the sprite that whisps and flutters around me and keeps me inspired to shoot for the moon – every day you grow and overcome some incredible odds in such a short time makes me stronger and keeps me writing to encourage and inspire the daughters of other parents of color.

When it comes down to it, the most important people that I need to thank for helping me get this book written are the ones whose experiences, challenges and victories inform this book. That includes my wonderful coaching community that consists of clients, grads, those who follow me on my social media platforms publically, as well as my private online network for like-minded leaders SLAYNET as well as those many organizations who have hired me to speak or conduct workshops for their talented leaders. It is within those conversations with the leaders themselves that I learn of topics that require deeper exploration, their pain points, the things that keep them up at night and the issues that keep them on guard.

I'd like to thank my team. They keep me buttoned up, looking and sounding good every day: Joy Y. Fernandez, Carmen Gamble, Leah Frazier, Andy Baeza, as well as my editorial and production team.

A special thanks to the Horowitz group for sharing their research with me and the Executive Leadership Council for sharing their insights and data as well as their platform with me as I facilitate workshops, speak and coach Fortune 500 executives in their institute.

Finally, a special thank you to my dear friend Valorie Burton, who continues to be my friend and inspiration in writing, coaching and leadership. I can always count on you to be on call via text to answer any questions and encourage me on this journey.

***

ABOUT THE AUTHOR

L. Michelle Smith is the CEO/founder of no silos communications LLC, a media and consulting company that develops high-performing executive leaders. She has more than 25 years as a leader in corporate America and small business.

Credentialed by the ICF, she runs a private, international coaching and consulting practice where she works with executives and organizations to create experiences that inspire exceptional leadership. She specializes in moving mid-level and GMs through senior executive leaders to the C-Suite and co-creating opportunities for C-Suite leaders to have lasting impact at their companies and industries. These leaders have hailed from American Express, Microsoft, Amazon, Google, Bank of America, AT&T, Lenovo, Netflix, Warner Media, CNN, Merck, Capital One and even some of the most recognizable organizations in the arts. She is also an adjunct faculty member and go-to executive coach for the Executive Leadership Council (ELC).

Yes Please! 7 Ways to Say I'm Entitled to the C-Suite

L. Michelle is also the author of the award-winning and best-selling *No Thanks: 7 Ways to Say I'll Just Include Myself: A Guide to Rockstar Leadership for Women of Color in the Workplace* (two editions) and the companion journal, *Slay Everyday: 52 Weeks to Rockstar Leadership*. She holds editing credit for her daughter's children's book *No Thanks for Girls: 7 Ways to Say I'm Beautiful, Strong & Enough*. She is also the creator, executive producer and host of The Culture Soup Podcast®, heard in more than 70 countries.

***

Made in the USA
Monee, IL
23 September 2023

12e15aeb-3bf0-4475-b68f-e84ed16a204cR01